Scandinavia
in World Politics

Europe Today
Series Editor: Ronald Tiersky

Scandinavia in World Politics

Christine Ingebritsen

ROWMAN & LITTLEFIELD PUBLISHERS, INC.
Lanham · Boulder · New York · Toronto · Oxford

ROWMAN & LITTLEFIELD PUBLISHERS, INC.

Published in the United States of America
by Rowman & Littlefield Publishers, Inc.
A wholly owned subsidiary of The Rowman & Littlefield Publishing Group, Inc.
4501 Forbes Boulevard, Suite 200, Lanham, Maryland 20706
www.rowmanlittlefield.com

P.O. Box 317, Oxford OX2 9RU, UK

British Library Cataloguing in Publication Information Available

Library of Congress Cataloging-in-Publication Data
Ingebritsen, Christine.
  Scandinavia in world politics / Christine Ingebritsen.
      p. cm. — (Europe today)
  Includes bibliographical references and index.
  ISBN-13: 978-0-7425-0965-8 (cloth : alk. paper)
  ISBN-10: 0-7425-0965-6 (cloth : alk. paper)
  ISBN-13: 978-0-7425-0966-5 (pbk. : alk. paper)
  ISBN-10: 0-7425-0966-4 (pbk. : alk. paper)
  1. States, Small. 2. Scandinavia—Foreign relations. I. Title. II. Series: Europe today
(Rowman and Littlefield, Inc.)
JC365.I54 2006
327.48—dc22

                                                                    2005035523

Printed in the United States of America

⊚ ™ The paper used in this publication meets the minimum requirements of
American National Standard for Information Sciences—Permanence of Paper
for Printed Library Materials, ANSI/NISO Z39.48-1992.

Dedicated to my children, CJ and Kari

Contents

Acknowledgments

The author wishes to thank Brewster Denny, Eric Einhorn, Katherine Hanson, Peter Katzenstein, Audie Klotz, Paulette Kurzer, Terje Leiren, Susan McEachern, Jonathan Mercer, Iver Neumann, TJ Pempel, Jonas Pontusson, Timothy Raines, Thomas Risse, Hans Peter Schmitz, Sidney Tarrow, Baldur Thorhallsson, Ron Tiersky; three University of Washington research assistants, Vaishali Kushan, Tom Smith, and Reinier Voorwinde; the participants in the graduate seminar Modern Scandinavian Politics, SCAND/POLISCI 519; and two anonymous reviewers for their valuable input during the completion of this project.

· 1 ·

Scandinavia in World Politics

$\mathcal{S}$candinavia and Scandinavians have consistently played important yet underestimated roles in world politics. Notable for their quiet success in world markets and recognized as a peaceful corner of northern Europe, these states exercise collective authority beyond their borders that exceeds their military or economic might. If we look at which citizens in the world today are involved in promoting new forms of conflict resolution, working to reduce global poverty, and seeking to strengthen international institutions, more likely than not we will find a team of Scandinavians.

Although small powers from Canada to the Netherlands may also seek to structure the rules of the game in international politics, patterns of economic dependence, political rivalries, religious differences, and problems of legitimacy have limited the capacity of many small states to play a global agenda-setting role. Thus, the focus of this analysis is the anomaly of Scandinavia's reputation building in critical areas of public diplomacy, recognizing the challenges to international legitimacy emanating from profound changes that are occurring within these societies.

There are four possible options for exercising influence in world politics. One means of exerting power is unilateralism. This is typically practiced by those members of the international system that possess power greater than all others, or hegemons. The United States now holds this unique position in global politics that Britain once held. Actions taken by hegemons have ripple effects throughout the world. The relative power of the hegemon also implies obligations—from preserving open seas for trade to averting war. As an actor's position in the world changes, it becomes increasingly difficult to act independently in world politics.

1

A second way to exert authority is through a partnership agreement with another member of the international community. When the Soviet military buildup on the Kola Peninsula appeared threatening, the Norwegian government negotiated a special treaty with the United States to pre-position materiel above the Arctic Circle in northern Norway. The 1981 U.S.-Norwegian agreement and U.S.–European Union (EU) cooperation to combat terrorism are examples of bilateral cooperation.

Another means of influence is through aligning with other governments, or multilateralism. Members of the international system promote their views and protect their interests by teaming up with others. Since the 1950s, Scandinavian intergovernmental cooperation (the Nordic Council) has deepened ties and provided a forum for collective action in world politics. Multilateralism has become increasingly attractive to Europeans as governments agree to collective policy making (European integration) to promote wealth and to influence global agenda setting. By being at the table, more influence is possible.

A fourth way to exert influence in international politics relies on the power of ideas. Actors adopting this means of influence focus all their resources on a particular issue or problem, with the intent of altering the international policy agenda. In this capacity, Scandinavia has emerged as a moral superpower by continuously and consistently advocating compliance with global standards of conduct and by working to develop, refine, and maintain principles of mutual understanding in world politics. Prominent representatives from these societies serve as transnational agenda-setters and provide leadership in generating new ideas within international institutions. And at home, Scandinavia provides examples of how power and wealth can be distributed more equitably; how gender and class differences can be minimized; and how state authority can be used in a positive way to temper markets and social injustice. These innovations have led sociologists, economists, political scientists, and environmental experts to study and import ideas from Scandinavian societies. By representing what is possible to achieve domestically and serving as transnational activists, Scandinavians and the foreign policy community strengthen codes of conduct or norms in international society. Even though Scandinavia is not always virtuous, and some Scandinavians are stronger leaders in agenda setting than others, as this book will argue, Scandinavians and members of these societies play the role of norm entrepreneurs in world politics. The historic evolution of Scandinavia's role and the consequences of taking on issues of social justice in global politics will be critically examined in the chapters to follow.

First, let us consider some contemporary examples of Scandinavia's agenda-setting role in world politics. The evidence of Scandinavian activism is striking. When Nelson Mandela, the leader of the anti-apartheid movement in

South Africa, was released from prison in 1990, he made his first international trip to Sweden. He deliberately visited Sweden to express his thanks for their efforts to end a system of government based on race. As South Africa worked for internal peace and conflict resolution, the Nobel Committee awarded Mandela and F. W. de Klerk (the then president of South Africa who lifted the ban on Mandela's anti-apartheid party) the prestigious Peace Prize in 1993.

When George W. Bush became president of the United States in 2001, Norwegian minister of the environment Siri Bjerke encouraged the U.S. government to abide by the global treaty on the environment, the Kyoto Protocol. The United States has refused to comply with the Kyoto agreement and failed to adopt restrictions on carbon emissions, much to the dismay of the international community. In contrast, the Scandinavians have cultivated a niche as a group of societies that have a long-held tradition of practicing sustainable development and represent an alternative model of eco-capitalism.

When international comparisons of poverty assistance are made, the Scandinavians consistently head the list of the most generous contributors. In 1995, Denmark contributed $311 per capita to developing nations, whereas the United States contributed only $28 per capita. Scandinavians target the poorest nations in the world and view this as appropriate preventive action against war and human suffering.

Scandinavians are strong advocates of adherence to principles of human rights and interpret their global responsibilities broadly. As stated by the Finnish government, "the principle of universality directly predicates the right and duty of the international community to override the principle of national sovereignty in promoting human rights and preventing violations of human rights all over the world."[1] As evidence of the Scandinavian commitment to promoting human rights in foreign policy making, these states have incorporated economic, social, and cultural rights in bilateral aid to developing countries.

Scandinavia has also been widely recognized as a leader in promoting gender equality and is regularly honored by prominent international organizations such as Save the Children and the United Nations. For example, Norway's commitment to national health care and investments in women's health has correlated with fewer incidences of death in pregnancy or childbirth than in the United States. And in international health care policy, former Norwegian prime minister Gro Harlem Brundtland initiated a new global agenda as the leader of the World Health Organization (WHO) by focusing attention and resources on the health of women.

In 2003, the Norwegian and Swedish governments adopted legislation to promote higher levels of female participation on company boards, a traditionally male-dominated domain. These measures set an international precedent and express shared values of equality and fair representation.

Prominent Scandinavian women have played a leading role in agenda setting in the UN. Bodil Begtrup (Denmark) helped create a UN Commission on the Status of Women in 1946 and worked on the text of the Universal Declaration of Human Rights (1947–1948).[2] Aase Lionaes (Norway) devoted her energies to establishing UN mechanisms for assisting refugees and worked tirelessly to promote the status of women. Alva Myrdal (Sweden) worked with the International Labor Organization (ILO) and the United Nations Educational, Scientific and Cultural Organizations (UNESCO) and consistently raised awareness of the interests of women.[3] As Doris Linder argues,

> politically experienced as a result of participation in non-governmental organizations and electoral politics, Scandinavian women delegates to the United Nations General Assembly used their political skills to help formulate and gain the adoption of resolutions, declarations, and conventions. Among them were the conventions on political rights and on the legal rights of women, and the declaration on the Elimination of Discrimination against Women—steps in the development of international norms for women's equality.[4]

As the UN drafted a Convention against Torture and other Cruel, Inhuman or Degrading Treatment or Punishment, the Swedes worked behind the scenes to bring parties to the table and to establish the norm advocated by Amnesty International: "The Swedish UN delegation initiated work on a convention by organizing broad co-sponsorship of an authorizing resolution that was adopted by the UN General Assembly."[5]

As the United States engaged in a controversial policy of military intervention in Iraq, UN weapons inspector Hans Blix (Sweden) emerged as a global critic of American strategy and an advocate for alternative response(s) to the challenges of nation building in the region, relying on principles of multilateral cooperation. The position of Scandinavia in international politics permits these societies and their leaders to provoke debate and suggest alternatives when larger powers exert their influence. These are just a few examples of Scandinavians involved in global agenda setting and norm entrepreneurship.

What makes Scandinavia unique, and how and why has Scandinavia developed a special role in foreign policy making? "Scandinavia" refers to the five northern European states (Denmark, Finland, Iceland, Norway, and Sweden) and the three territories of Greenland, the Faroes, and Åaland Island. The entire population of this subregion of Europe is only 24.5 million (see table 1.1).

With fewer ambassadors to send abroad and limited resources as states with relatively small populations, Scandinavia and representatives from these societies pursue a specific set of tasks in international politics. Foreign

Table 1.1.   The Population of Scandinavia

Denmark	5.4 million
Finland	5.2 million
Iceland	290,000
Norway	4.6 million
Sweden	8.9 million
The Three Territories	
Åland	26,000
Faroes	48,000
Greenland	57,000

Source: Nordic Council. *Nordic Statistical Yearbook 2004* (Copenhagen: Nordic Council of Ministers), p. 61.

ministry officials work with a designated list of priorities, or portfolios. However, Scandinavia's role is both objective (the content of the statements, documents, and actions of the foreign policy–making community) and subjective (dependent on how others see them). As Jonathan Mercer states, reputations exist in the minds of observers.[6]

One thing that is notable about Scandinavia is its transformation from being a zone of hostility to one of tranquility. Scandinavia no longer inspires fear from its neighbors and is instead the site where the Nobel Peace Prize is awarded. How did this situation evolve, and what were some of the important historic moments in the development of a group of like-minded northern European social welfare states?

Scandinavia has not always been a peaceful, harmonious corner of Europe. During the Viking Age (793–1066 A.D.), warriors from Scandinavia earned a reputation for brutality. According to an English priest who described an attack on a monastery on the northeastern coast of England, "pagans from the north came with a naval force to Britain like stinging hornets and spread on all sides like fearful wolves, robbed, tore and slaughtered not only beasts of burden, sheep and oxen, but even priests and deacons."[7]

Vikings had a global presence before the term globalization (intensified interaction between markets, polities, and societies) became prominent. Vikings were Scandinavians who attacked, traded with, or settled in territories throughout Europe, east into Russia, south to the Mediterranean, and west to North America. Relying on superior technology (boat building), a high degree of organization (such as legal codes and rules of engagement), and sheer physical strength, Vikings are associated with power to the present day.

In 840 A.D., Vikings launched a series of notorious attacks—ransacking cities such as Hamburg, Rouen, Chartres, and Tours. The Vikings also attacked the city of Paris, occupying both banks of the Seine. After receiving a sizable sum of silver, the Vikings moved on to hold positions in the French countryside.[8] Vikings ventured to Portugal (844) and to Provence and Tuscany (859–862)[9] and occupied the outer islands—from the Orkneys, the Faroes, and the Hebrides to Ireland. Knut the Dane ruled the North Sea region, from Denmark to England, and for two hundred years the Vikings waged numerous battles throughout the northern area. Yet Viking influence was not limited to the area we now refer to as Scandinavia—these oarsmen had a global presence.

According to historical evidence, Vikings headed to North America and established a settlement known as Vinland, in the northern area of Newfoundland.[10] Vikings colonized Iceland and Greenland and controlled much of England (from Yorkshire to the Thames) until their defeat at Stamford Bridge in 1066. Known for their brutality and strategic maneuvers (such as launching surprise attacks on holy days), Vikings were a feared lot. According to legend, prayers were said throughout Europe during this period: "Save us, O Lord, from the fury of the Northmen."[11]

Scandinavians were not only brutal warriors overseas, but also inflicted severe casualties in battles with one another. Although united under a single monarch in the Kalmar Union, the two kingdoms of Sweden and Denmark fought fierce battles for control of southern Sweden and the Baltic Sea area. One of many such incidents occurred in 1520. The "Stockholm Bloodbath," with a death toll of eighty-two victims, was a brutal outcome of this longstanding Danish-Swedish rivalry during the reign of Christian II of Denmark. Christian beheaded his opponents in order to retain control and protect his ascendancy to power.

In addition to establishing a reputation as tough fighters, Scandinavians were also early competitors in international markets. Swedes established trade routes deep into Russia and into the Byzantine Empire during the Viking Age. Bergen (Norway) became an important center in German-dominated trade between European city-states, as part of the Hanseatic League founded in the twelfth century. In the 1400s, the Danes found it lucrative to charge all ships sailing to and from the Baltic "Sound dues." This profitable venture lasted over four hundred years. Impressed by the international success of the Dutch in international trade, the Danes brought Dutch peasants to Copenhagen in the sixteenth century to teach techniques of the farm trade.[12]

How did these great warriors of the north and fierce traders become a model of peaceful cooperation in world politics? In *Viking Age Iceland*, Jesse Byock demonstrates the importance of legal codes in establishing boundaries of authority and guiding social relations. Early respect for legal authority created more egalitarianism *within* these societies, according to Scandinavian scholars. Icelandic feuds were settled by courts of law, and "Icelanders consistently acted with restraint."[13] Although legal mechanisms did not eliminate conflict in these societies, evidence of cooperation took unique forms. Even during the Viking Age, the division of property was decided according to common principles, rights of women were delineated, and boundaries of appropriate and inappropriate conduct were established in law and in custom. For example, when a whale washed ashore on the Icelandic coastline, the community shared this resource, and it provided wealth to the entire community, not the individual farmer or fisherman. Collaboration and establishment of norms of cooperation have become associated with "Scandinavianism." Even when the capacity to retain these agreements is untenable, it has become a common practice to promote cooperative solutions.

The Kalmar Union is a stunning example of cross-national cooperation that was negotiated by Scandinavian royalty in the fourteenth century. Under the reign of Queen Margaret of Denmark, the leaders of Scandinavia met in Kalmar, Sweden, in 1397, where plans were drawn for a closer union among the monarchs. Margaret's son, Erik of Pomerania, was named king of Scandinavia (Denmark, Norway, and Sweden) at Kalmar, and the three realms committed themselves to far-reaching forms of collaboration, from a common defense policy and mutual recognition of outlaws to a pledge to remain unified under one crown. The Kalmar Union could not be sustained, nor was power equally shared within the union. Sweden and Norway were subordinated to Denmark, and Copenhagen became the center of power during the Kalmar Union. Erik followed Margaret's foreign policy and countered German power, while imposing high taxes on Sweden and Norway. The Swedish nobility withdrew from the union, but Norway was too weak to become fully independent from Danish authority. Even though the union broke apart in 1523, it remains a historic benchmark of regional cooperation, symbolized by the three crowns.

What had been a partnership evolved into warring factions during the first half of the seventeenth century. As Swedish leaders sought control of Scandinavia, King Christian IV of united Denmark-Norway unsuccessfully attempted to counter growing Swedish power. However, by 1700, Sweden had become the great power of the north under King Karl XII, an ambitious leader of military campaigns who reigned from 1699–1718. Swedish authority extended into Poland, and eventually led to a Swedish-Polish alliance against Russia. In 1709, Karl's force was defeated by Peter the Great; Sweden's expansion to the east ended in Poltava.

Political expansion and military engagement had weakened Scandinavia's monarchies as these societies entered the age of Enlightenment. New ideas, human discoveries, and a growing respect for expert knowledge, such as the most effective way to grow the potato or distill aquavit, challenged traditional authority structures. Population growth and the expansion of industry gradually changed the composition of Scandinavian societies. Absolute monarchs tolerated the rise of a new political class of leaders in the eighteenth century and eventually lost their hold over these societies.

By 1809, Scandinavians began to establish constitutional arrangements and legal mechanisms to counter royal power. A domestic institution-building process took priority over military engagements. As these states entered the modern era, the people and governments of Scandinavia developed a civilized reputation in foreign and domestic politics.

Karl Deutsch referred to Scandinavia as a "security community": a group of states where the prospect of waging war has become unthinkable. The taming of the Vikings occurred over several centuries; so, too were the ambitions of kings and queens subordinated to the will of the people. Although this occurred elsewhere in Europe, it took a distinct path still apparent today in Scandinavian domestic and international politics.

THE EMERGENCE OF A SECURITY COMMUNITY

After 1814, Scandinavia no longer initiated armed conflict with neighboring states. The focus turned inward, to resolving conflict between different power centers within these societies. As Norway was transferred from the Danish crown to the Swedish crown (rewarding the Swedish king Bernadotte for turning his back on Napoleon), Prince Christian Frederik of Norway received sage advice from his older cousin, King Frederik VI of Denmark in a letter, March 21, 1814: "endeavor to uphold Norway's independence, see to it that Norway obtain from the King of Sweden such terms as will allow of Norway's becoming a federative state under the Swedish King."[14] National leaders met at Eidsvoll to draft a constitution in the spring of 1814. The Basic Law for the Kingdom of Norway provided the foundations for an autonomous nation. The Swedish king and the Norwegian Parliament agreed to accept the terms of the Swedish-Norwegian union, which would last until 1905.

In nineteenth-century Sweden, the existing governing structures were unable to accommodate the rise of a new middle class, and citizens demanded reforms. Large demonstrations protested the retention of power by the king, and decades of debate over how the society should be ruled ensued.[15] When the king tried to shut down Sweden's first political newspaper, *Aftonbladet*, the publisher refused to comply. Symbolizing the end of an era of absolute rule, the call for reform intensified. After much debate, in 1866 a system of four estates (the knighthood and nobility, the clergy, the burghers, and the peasants) was replaced by a two-chamber parliament (the Riksdag).[16] The members of the nobility served in the first chamber, whereas the second chamber was overwhelmingly made up of farmers.

In the same period, the beginnings of the "organized society" started to take shape. Norway's first major interest organization (Friends of the Farmers) was established in the 1860s. A coalition of farmers joined with Johan Sverdrup, a lawyer and academic, to challenge the authority of the king's power in policy making. The resolution of the conflict between the king and parliament was settled in 1884, when the king invited Sverdrup to form a government based on the strength of his support in the parliament. This is the practice for forming a new government to the present day.[17] Across the border in Sweden, agrarian interests also mobilized and became important factors in shaping national politics. In 1914, farmers came by the thousands to protest the government's defense policy. Two separate parties were created to represent Swedish farmers and incorporate their voices in the policy-making process.

As Scandinavia strengthened its version of participatory democracy and royal power declined, other movements gained momentum—from the rights of workers, universal suffrage, equality of the sexes, to independence (Norway from Sweden, Finland from Russia, Iceland from Denmark). Yet, in most cases, conflicts were peacefully resolved by the creation of collective organizations and the subordination of violence to newly created institutions. Organizations were created to represent new groups in society, which had the effect of mitigating social unrest. These included national federations of labor unions, national employer federations, leagues of feminists, and national labor parties founded on principles of socialism.

In contrast to other societies, border disputes were negotiated without resorting to violence. When the national independence movement gathered momentum at the end of the 1800s in Norway, and political leaders announced the formation of a new government, the break-up of the Swedish-Norwegian union occurred in 1905 without the outbreak of armed conflict or disputes over territorial boundaries. Several decades later, Iceland broke away peacefully from Denmark (1944)—this occurred during Germany's occupation of Denmark, and the Danes were unable to prevent Icelandic independence. Only in Finland did the transition from a Russian duchy to an independent Finnish nation-state lead to an outbreak of civil war. In each instance when Scandinavians relinquished authority to another part of Scandinavia, conflict was averted.

Scandinavia experienced the social pressures of urbanization and industrialization in the nineteenth century, yet avoided the types of political rebellions that occurred elsewhere in Europe during this period. According to historians, mass emigration from Scandinavia to America provided a safety valve and prevented groups in these societies from mobilizing against political authorities. Between 1860 and 1914, approximately one million people left Sweden (nearly one-fourth of the population). A similar exodus occurred across the border in neighboring Norway. Marcus Thrane, the head of the Norwegian labor organization, had had revolutionary ideas. As argued by Terje Leiren, by the time of Thrane's arrest and subsequent emigration to the United States, the threat of his group emulating revolutions elsewhere in Europe had dissipated.

In the modern era, Scandinavia has led the way in seeking innovative, multilateral solutions and has collectively intervened to strengthen codes of conduct in international politics.[18] For example, in 1880, the Norwegian Parliament (the Storting) actively supported international arbitration. By incorporating a voice for labor unions within the party system and by establishing a system of labor negotiations with management, the Scandinavians developed an innovative way to cope with industrial disputes. Although scholars have demonstrated how the power of labor has weakened in relation to business (see, for example, Jonas Pontusson, *The Limits of Social Democracy*), Scandinavians still enjoy more free time away from the job, higher levels of protection from health and safety risks, and more protection from the inequalities of market forces than people in other advanced industrial countries. The innovativeness of Scandinavians continues—even amid tremendous pressures to reform political institutions at home. Yet these practices are rarely considered in studies of comparative foreign-policy making.

Scandinavia also became noteworthy for acting earlier than larger, more powerful actors in the international community on many environmental and social issues. In the 1800s, Finland established restrictions on the timber industry, an early example of environmental regulation. Finland was also among the first nations in the world to grant the vote to women. In Iceland, the founding of the Red Stocking Party in the 1920s represented the first party in the world devoted to women's issues. The Norwegian parliament established progressive social legislation for workers and families early in the twentieth century. In the 1930s, the ascendance of the Swedish Social Democrats ushered in an era of progressive social policies under the leadership of Per Albin Hanson. And the desire for equality extended to equal representation in the national legislature, as indicated in the 1948 election campaign slogan in Sweden: "Without women, no democratic governance."

During the tense years of the Cold War, Scandinavia was strategically vulnerable; however, these governments consistently implemented innovative diplomatic measures to dissipate conflict between the two opposing blocs. By inviting great power leaders to their capitals as sites for conflict mediation and institution building (from Stockholm's 1972 UN Conference on the Environment to the Reykjavik Summit between Reagan and Gorbachev) and by meeting with leaders in Washington, D.C., and Moscow, Scandinavia cultivated an international role against superior military might.

Ideational leadership and transnational activism continue to be defining features of Scandinavian foreign policy making. And changes in world politics have provided new possibilities (as well as new challenges) for norm entrepreneurship in an era of intensified global political, economic, and social interaction.

SCANDINAVIA TODAY

With the unraveling of the Cold War system of opposing blocs, Scandinavia engages a complicated set of global problems, and, as in an earlier historical period, these governments have put forward alternative models of engagement. Not all solutions advocated by northern Europeans are adopted by more powerful states, nongovernmental organizations (NGOs), or international organizations. Yet Scandinavia continues to cultivate its distinctiveness in the global arena—even during a period of domestic transformation. Precisely because of the legacy of its unique institutions, policies, and ideas, Scandinavia is well suited to exercise moral authority in world politics.

Why Scandinavia? Scandinavia has been viewed as a social laboratory, notable for innovative and progressive forms of state intervention in the society and the economy. In these democratic systems, interest groups are included in national policy–making decisions, as opposed to being outside the corridors of power. Workers have historically enjoyed more authority over the terms of their employment than elsewhere through a set of unique institutions and policies. The capacity for cooperation between political parties (the Agrarians and the Social Democrats) established the well-known, compassionate welfare state—providing social welfare benefits above and beyond the United Kingdom, the United States, and Continental Europe. These innovations have brought external attention and prominence to Scandinavia.

What about the crisis of the Scandinavian model? In recent decades, scholars such as Jonas Pontusson have documented the "end of the third road," referring to the political, economic, and ideological crises of Scandinavian social democracy—particularly in Sweden. As Paul Pierson and Karen Anderson declare, the leading Scandinavian welfare state is no longer in a position of expansion, but instead the government engages in reforming the social policies and cutting back on its generous programs. Nonetheless, as Bo

Rothstein argues in *Just Institutions Matter*, the core values and institutions of Sweden's welfare state have remained remarkably resilient in the face of domestic and international challenges. Across the border in Norway, the welfare system is undergoing reforms yet has abundant reserves from unprecedented petroleum prosperity. Scandinavians remain committed to the provision of universal benefits and to playing a role in international society consistent with the golden age of welfare capitalism.

How can Scandinavia influence the international system? Scandinavia's influence on world politics is multifaceted. Prominent individuals exported from these societies have governed international institutions. For example, Trygve Lie (from Norway) served as the first secretary-general of the UN and Dag Hammarskjold (from Sweden) helped shape the form and substance of this multilateral institution. Gro Harlem Brundtland brought years of experience and leadership within the Norwegian Social Democratic Party to her role as the director of WHO. Swedish prime minister Carl Bildt wrote a formative article in *Foreign Affairs* entitled "The Baltic Litmus Test," challenging the West to stabilize conditions in Russia by reaching out and cooperating with the three Baltic States, Estonia, Latvia, and Lithuania. Bildt has also been invited to mediate conflicts at the request of more powerful states— as a trusted partner, with the reputation of being a Swedish internationalist.

Scandinavians also pursue common agendas, building on the cultural and political ties these governments and societies have forged collectively. For example, Scandinavia cooperates formally (through participation in the intergovernmental Nordic Council) and informally (through its delegations to international organizations such as the UN) to pursue common goals in international politics. During critical moments in international politics, prominent Scandinavians have served as the conscience of larger powers. Swedish prime minister Olof Palme spoke out against American intervention in Vietnam and worked actively for disarmament during the height of the Cold War. Domestic innovations also serve to guide other societies and create a sense of what is possible elsewhere—from gender equality in politics, environmental regulations, legal protections for children, and government efforts to counter bullying. Electoral politics in Scandinavia enable these societies to keep their agendas consistent, with important demonstration effects on other societies. The largest political party in northern Europe, the Social Democrats, has repeatedly been returned to office, providing continuity in policy making and enhanced international experience to teams of norm entrepreneurs.

Recent changes in these societies have brought into question many of the institutions and policies established under the prominence of the Social Democratic Party, Scandinavia's leading political party. Ten of the most important changes in the Scandinavian way are outlined in table 1.2. These

Table 1.2. Ten Important Changes in Scandinavian Societies

1. The emergence of rival producers (similar goods, lower prices)
2. The revival of cooperation in Europe since the 1980s
3. Growing perception that Scandinavia is no longer better off than the rest of Europe
4. Challenges to national identity associated with growing diversity
5. Adjusting to life after the Cold War—new threats to security
6. Reforming the welfare state is the priority—not expansion
7. Higher levels of joblessness
8. A growing acceptance of privatization as appropriate
9. Mergers and acquisitions between flagship Scandinavian firms and multinational companies
10. The ascendance of single-issue protest parties

include living with higher levels of unemployment; the economic, political, and cultural effects of globalization; and the integration of Scandinavia's largest trading partner, the EU.

The two most difficult challenges facing Scandinavia today are the transfer of authority away from Scandinavia to the EU, as regional integration continues to deepen, and the influx of non-Scandinavian immigrants. Scandinavia has traditionally preferred autonomy to integration, and, until recently, has remained more aloof from European political cooperation. Yet, in today's Europe, Scandinavia is increasingly bound by decisions made outside the territorial boundaries of these societies—a difficult political reality that requires new types of partnerships and, in many instances, a change in the way Scandinavia has organized its own institutions and policies.

Immigration threatens Scandinavia's "ideology of social partnership," one of the defining features of political institutions in northern Europe (see Katzenstein 1985). For societies where there is one way of celebrating Christmas, the introduction of new languages, cuisines, and religious practices is threatening to many and tolerated by others. Scandinavian societies are politically divided over the immigration question. As public support for anti-immigration parties gains momentum and incidences of hate crimes receive international attention, these pose threats to Scandinavia's reputation of being the conscience of international society.

The evolution of the Scandinavian model of welfare capitalism is a continuous and ongoing political process, and so is the pursuit of global objectives in world politics. Scandinavians persistently promote their vision(s) of the good society—in relations with other Europeans and in global agenda setting. Thus, even though the Scandinavian model has had to change at home, these societies actively seek to export the model abroad—to the region and to the globe. In the absence of extensive military power or the capacity to determine prices in global markets, Scandinavia cultivates its role as a global good citizen.

How do Scandinavians play this role? Scandinavia and prominent members of these societies provide moral leadership and do so through a diversity of channels. One important example of moral leadership is the announcement each year of the recipient(s) of the Nobel Peace Prize. First awarded in 1901 according to the will left by Swedish inventor Alfred Nobel, the prize is a decision left to a committee appointed by the Norwegian parliament because of his respect for that institution. By awarding the Nobel Peace Prize, a committee of five Norwegians determines which groups or individuals should be recognized for their international efforts to promote peace and security in world politics. There is no equivalent award made by more powerful states or regional institutions, and Scandinavian choices represent a normative statement about the direction of global society. The prize is often awarded with the intent to advance a particular agenda at a critical moment in world politics.

Nobel Peace Prize recipients include Jean Henri Dunant, founder of the International Committee of the Red Cross (1901); Woodrow Wilson, founder of the League of Nations (1919); Fridtjof Nansen, originator of the Nansen passports for refugees (1922); Ferdinand Buisson, founder of the League of Human Rights (1927); Jane Addams, president of the Women's International League for Peace and Freedom (1931); Carl Von Ossietzky, German pacifist (1936); Cordell Hull for his work in establishing the UN (1945); Georges Pire, leader of the relief organization for refugees (1958); Martin Luther King, leader of the Southern Christian Leadership Conference (1964); Rene Cassin, president of the European Court of Human Rights (1968); Amnesty International (1977); Anwar Al-Sadat, president of Egypt, and Menachem Begin, president of Israel (1978); Lech Walesa, founder of Polish Solidarity movement (1983); Nelson Mandela and Frederik W. de Klerk (1993); International Campaign to Ban Landmines and Jody Williams, campaign organizer (1997); the United Nations and Kofi Annan (2001); Jimmy Carter (2002); Shirin Edabij, Iranian human rights activist (2003); African environmental leader Wangari Maathai (2004); and Mohamed El Baradei of the International Atomic Energy Agency (IAEA) (2005).

The Nobel Committee selects international nominations according to specific criteria, but it makes the final decision. Its decision is often controversial. Thus, the Nobel Peace Prize is a small hammer used by Scandinavians (in this case, a committee of five Norwegians) to send a message about desired outcomes in world politics.

In their efforts to structure the global agenda, Scandinavian governments actively pursue the strengthening of the UN and other forms of collective security, the protection of human rights and the environment, the elimination of poverty, and the reduction of global armaments. They have done so not just with words but also with their actions. These are logical international commitments, given an understanding of the development of domestic institutions and policies.

Therefore, even though the Scandinavian model of the good society is under attack in domestic politics, exporting the legacy of Scandinavian innovations remains a primary task of foreign policy makers. Gro Harlem Brundtland refers to her role in world politics as "building an international public sector," which reflects the benign attitude of her generation of social democrats regarding the role of the state in society. As the following analysis suggests, Scandinavia's role has become even more appropriate as new challenges confront the international community.

Scandinavian motives may sound purely altruistic—however, their role in world politics also may be viewed as strategic. Smaller states cannot afford to have disruptions in trade or market access, for it is too costly for them. These economies and their exports benefit from favorable reputations in world markets. For example, the Swedish automotive company Volvo has cultivated a global image as a safe vehicle. Other products are associated with good health, fitness, and energy efficiency. For Scandinavians, idealism is not only a good way of exercising influence, but it also protects (and expands) market shares. Thus, for small states, it is strategic to be virtuous in world politics.

OVERVIEW OF THE BOOK

This chapter outlines Scandinavia's unique role in the world today. Once feared and now respected in international politics, this corner of Europe cultivates a good reputation through multiple means: by exporting ideas abroad; through persistent leadership in international regime development (from global aid to the environment); by pursuing novel solutions at home; by exporting prominent representatives of these societies to govern international institutions; by shaming those who violate norms; and by awarding the Nobel Prize in recognition of global excellence in the pursuit of peace.

Chapter two discusses the origins of Scandinavian exceptionalism and the political, social, and economic changes that have led many observers to question whether Scandinavia remains a model society. Four cultural experiences shaped the development of Scandinavian societies: rural settlement patterns, the role of religion, economic dependence on natural resources, and reliance on constitutions as legitimate means of authority. Chapter two examines the paradox of the "crisis" of the Scandinavian model and the relationship between domestic politics and Scandinavia's international role. Even though institutions, policies, and values appear to have less solidarity in

Scandinavia today than in the past, this corner of Europe maintains an active presence, and members of these societies seek to structure the agenda in world politics.

Chapter three provides an analysis of Scandinavia's role within the EU. Since the accession of Sweden and Finland to the EU in 1995, more of the Scandinavian states are now members than nonmembers. Even Iceland and Norway, which have both decided not to join for the foreseeable future, are actively engaged in other forms of European cooperation and increasingly seek to have influence within EU circles. To what extent has the EU been influenced by the presence of more Scandinavians in its institutions and negotiating bodies? Under the Finnish (1999) and Swedish (2001) EU presidencies, these governments exercised an important role in the agenda-setting process. More emphasis has been given to the political stability of Russia and the Baltic States, to promoting and enforcing EU environmental standards, and to issues of employment and the transparency of EU institutions. In a different capacity, the Danes have also exerted their influence within European institutions. As a member since 1973, the Danish path to Europe has been much more resistant. The Danish voice within the EU represents the legacy of social democratic institutions—from promoting greater democracy to questioning the market-based orientation of EU cooperation to rejecting the European currency unit as an intrusion on the sovereignty of the state. Chapter three counters the assumption that small powers no longer have a role to play in an integrated Europe and provides evidence of Scandinavian influence within the EU.

Chapter four discusses Norway's niche in world politics. The Norwegians have abundant oil and natural gas resources, which (along with membership in the North Atlantic Treaty Organization, NATO) has corresponded to resistance to European Union membership. As a consequence of Norway's decision to reject EU membership, the government has retained greater flexibility to pursue an independent foreign policy. Thus, Norway is in a position to object to proposals raised by the EU, in contrast to its neighbors. When Norwegians met in Seattle, Washington, to engage in the World Trade Organization (WTO) negotiations, the delegation opposed the liberalization of agricultural subsidies endorsed by the EU. And in Middle East peace negotiations, Norwegians have greater autonomy to pursue their own course— outside the parameters of EU foreign-policy making. This has led to some important innovations in peace making. Norway was the first to establish the precedent of relying on NGOs to lay the groundwork for contacts between opposing parties. The conclusion of the Oslo Accord has become a model for global conflict resolution.

Norway also exercises defiance by promoting its own understanding of "sustainable development" in global environmental policy. Under the leadership of Prime Minister Gro Harlem Brundtland, the Norwegian government exercised a legal right to refrain from participation in the International Whaling Commission's ban on global whaling. Norway maintains a domestic tradition of coastal whaling that is viewed as uncivilized by other more powerful states. Norway seeks to remove the minke whale from the list of endangered species based on scientific evidence of abundant populations. In doing so, Norway cultivates its international reputation as a principled player in foreign policy making.

Chapter five outlines how Icelanders and Finns turn global challenges into opportunities. These two societies in different ways defy those who are pessimistic about the capacities of small states to survive in a competitive international system. The determination of the Finns to protect their territorial sovereignty in the Winter War against the Soviet Union and the transformation of the national forestry firm Nokia into a global competitor in the cellular phone industry are remarkable examples of what Finns call *"sisu"* (inner strength). Considered a special Finnish trait, *sisu* is associated with perserverance, endurance, and exceptional patience—particularly in sports and warfare.[19] In Iceland, the desire to be completely independent of fossil fuels and profit from the natural resources of the sea represents a departure from the development models of more powerful states (the EU and the United States). As argued by Baldur Thorhallsson, smaller administrations may permit a more efficient realization of select policy goals, as demonstrated in Iceland.

Chapter six examines the risks to Scandinavia's reputation in world politics. If Scandinavia fails to accommodate difference at home, it becomes more difficult to practice credible global diplomacy. The pressures on homogeneous societies are enormous. Yet the ways in which Scandinavians have engaged multiculturalism is troubling—from the election of an anti-immigrant party to power in Denmark to the growing societal debates in Norway, Sweden, and Finland over how to engage attitudes toward immigrants as separate and different from mainstream society. These issues remain unresolved, the problems continue to become more complex, and they are objects of international scrutiny. Our understanding of how the Scandinavian model will evolve is also under review, raising questions about the resilience of the universal welfare system and the consequences for the capacity of these societies to play the role of norm entrepreneurs.

Chapter seven explains how Scandinavia's prominence in global politics has been contingent on the role of norms. Global responses to the Kosovo crisis and to the composition of Austria's coalition government are representative of a new era in international politics. Diplomats are less concerned with issues of war and peace between states and more attentive to good conduct within states. In a global political system where virtue is rewarded, Scandinavia seeks to define what it means to be virtuous. Precisely because of its reputation for pursuing social justice and institutionalizing compromise between conflicting parties in their domestic politics, Scandinavia is well suited to be a player in new millennium global politics. These states and societies share legitimacy and moral authority as they seek to exercise influence in Europe and in international politics. Virtue is not equally recognized, and some Scandinavians have enjoyed more success than others in pursuing this global role.

With growing incidences of crime and challenges associated with assimilating immigrants in these societies, Scandinavia must also accept the responsibility of principled politics. In some cases, the consequences of playing the role of a norm leader may have a boomerang effect. Norway's threat from the al Qaeda terrorist organization and the assassination of the Swedish foreign minister Anna Lindh in 2003 are critical examples of how ideational politics may have repercussions at home. However, the continued willingness of this group of northern European societies to initiate and sustain a global role requires further examination as an unexplored dimension of how power is exercised in international relations.

NOTES

1. Finnish Ministry of Foreign Affairs, *Human Rights and Finland's Foreign Policy* (Helsinki: Edita, 2000), p. 10.

2. Doris H. Linder, "Equality for Women: The Contribution of Scandinavian Women at the United Nations, 1946–66," *Scandinavian Studies* 73 (Summer 2001): 165.

3. Linder, "Equality for Women," pp. 178–80.

4. Linder, "Equality for Women," p. 208.

5. Ann Marie Clark, *Diplomacy of Conscience: Amnesty International and Changing Human Rights Norms* (Princeton, NJ: Princeton University Press, 2001), p. 60.

6. See Jonathan Mercer, *Reputation and International Politics* (Ithaca, NY: Cornell University Press, 1996).

7. Ivar Libæk and Øyvind Stenersen, *A History of Norway: From the Ice Age to the Age of Petroleum* (Oslo: Grøndahl Dreyer, 1999), p. 18.

8. Yves Cohat, *The Vikings: Lords of the Seas* (New York: Harry N. Abrams, Inc., 1992), pp. 46–48.

9. Norman Davies, *Europe: A History* (Oxford: Oxford University Press, 1996), p. 293.

10. The area along the northern tip of Newfoundland is called "L'Anse aux Meadows" today.

11. Cohat, in *The Vikings*, asserts that this prayer was said throughout Europe in the eighth century. However, Scandinavian historian Terje Leiren refutes this (see

Leiren, *Marcus Thrane: A Norwegian Radical in America* [Northfield, MN: Norwegian American Historical Association, 1987]). There is no documentary evidence to sustain this. Nonetheless, it has become part of the legend associated with Viking power.

12. Palle Lauring, *A History of Denmark* (Copenhagen: Host and Sons Forlag, 1960), p. 126.

13. Jesse Byock, *Viking Age Iceland* (London: Penguin Books, 2001), p. 77.

14. Lauring, *A History of Denmark*, pp. 200–201.

15. Stig Hadenius, *The Riksdag in Focus: Swedish History in a Parliamentary Perspective* (Stockholm: Berlings Arlov, 1997).

16. Hadenius, *The Riksdag in Focus*, pp. 130–31.

17. Libæk and Stenersen, *A History of Norway*, 90–91.

18. Chris Reus-Smit in *The Moral Purpose of the State* (Princeton, NJ: Princeton University Press, 1999) examines the evolution of multilateralism in world politics—from "Geneva law" to universally accepted procedures that structure international politics following the Hague Conferences of 1899 and 1907.

19. Olli Alho, ed., *Finland: A Cultural Encyclopedia* (Helsinki: Finnish Literature Society, 1997), pp. 292–93.

· 2 ·

The Origins of Global Agenda Setting

$\mathcal{S}$candinavia has emerged as a global advocate for human rights, solidarity, peace, the environment, and equality. Prominent individuals, socialized within these systems, have played a leading role in promoting international activism in foreign-policy making. And Scandinavian governments consistently engage particular agendas in world politics with distinct policy goals. The countries of the northernmost corner of Europe have developed and cultivated an international reputation as good citizens in the global community.

Other small or medium-sized powers (from the Netherlands to Canada) pursue agendas in world politics similar to the Scandinavians. Yet, more often than not, global attention is drawn to the five northern European states because of historic innovations (the Nobel Peace Prize, leadership in foreign aid, environmental entrepreneurship, and pioneering gender equity practices).

This chapter explains how and why Scandinavia, in contrast to other parts of the world, plays the role of moral superpower by examining the origins of foreign-policy making. The following discussion addresses four questions: What are the defining characteristics of Scandinavian politics and society? How have Scandinavians exercised influence in international politics? How and why has Scandinavia experienced profound changes in recent decades? What do these changes mean for Scandinavia's reputation and capacity to play the role of "norm entrepreneurs" in world politics?

POLITICS AND SOCIETY

In Scandinavia, political power is vested in legislatures, or parliaments. Iceland has the world's oldest national assembly, the Althing, where leaders met to resolve conflict as early as 930 A.D. The members of the Swedish Riksdag, Norwegian Storting, Danish Folketing, Finnish Eduskunta, and Icelandic Althing are democratically elected by secret ballot. According to the constitutions of Sweden (1809), Norway (1814), Denmark (1849), Finland (1905), and Iceland (1944), the number of votes cast for a political party determines the proportion of representatives in the government.[1] The rules of representation vary—from 2 percent of the total votes (Denmark) to 4 percent of the total votes (Sweden). Iceland and Finland are republics, which divide the responsibilities of the executive between a president and a prime minister. The heads of government in Sweden, Denmark, and Norway are prime ministers, and in these societies monarchs serve a political function as symbols of the nation.

Scandinavian political systems rely on the input of organized interest groups. Policies are adopted after consulting with advocates from industry and representatives from the labor movement. This tripartite arrangement (government, labor, business) is also characteristic of other small European states (Belgium, Netherlands, Austria, and Switzerland).[2] However, Scandinavia's dependence on agriculture and the formation of independent farmers' parties created a particular Nordic polity—and, in some states (such as Norway), the highest levels of support for agriculture in Europe.

One political party has played a critical role in modern Scandinavia. The Social Democrats emerged as the leading political party in Scandinavia in the early twentieth century. Ideologically, the party has represented the working class in national politics and has adopted many of the concerns of the labor movement. In the 1930s, the Social Democratic Party adopted a full employment policy as part of its economic platform. Promoting peace and social justice (the promotion of economic equality and political rights) have also been central foreign policy concerns of the Social Democrats. When conflict escalated in Europe, a team of Social Democrats, including Thorvald Stauning, chair of the Danish party, and Hjalmar Branting from Sweden, cooperated with Pieter Troelsta from the Netherlands and invited a group of international socialists to a 1917 conference in Stockholm. The meeting explored ways to resolve the European conflict. The electoral success of the Social Democratic Party is legendary in Sweden, where between 1932 and 1991 the party consistently received at least 40 percent of the vote. Only in recent decades have other parties emerged to rival the Social Democrats in Scandinavian politics.

In comparison to other advanced democracies, Scandinavia's political systems established more comprehensive welfare states, providing "cradle to grave" benefits (infant stipends, family leave, support for childcare, support for education, health care, unemployment insurance, pensions, etc.) for *all* members of the society. To sustain this generous system, Scandinavian finance ministries have relied on income from user fees, income taxes, taxes levied on business, and export revenues.

The commitment of citizens to taking care of everyone in the society is unique, and has given Scandinavia an international reputation for its distinctive universal welfare system. In contrast to the United Kingdom, the United States, and Australia, there is no stigma associated with welfare provisions. And, unlike the rest of Europe, recipients of welfare are not required to be part of the workforce—it is an entitlement designed to protect those residing in Scandinavia from the uncertainty of market forces.

Many explanations for Scandinavian exceptionalism focus on the role of the Social Democratic parties in establishing universal welfare systems. Other scholars emphasize the path-dependent development of specific institutions unique to northern European societies. Yet another way of understanding Scandinavian politics and society relies on a rich understanding of the nation-building process and the defining moments that have shaped interests and identities.

Four cultural factors shaped Scandinavia's emergence as modern welfare states: rural values, the role of religion in society, economic dependence on natural resources, and the adoption of constitutions delineating the boundaries of political authority. In contrast to the more urban, industrialized societies of Continental Europe, Scandinavia's political and social development was shaped by traditions of life in the countryside. These societies share an agrarian heritage, and during the period of serfdom, peasants in Scandinavia remained independent with greater control over their land than peasants elsewhere. Scandinavian urbanization and industrialization came later than in the rest of Europe, and, despite social unrest, these transformations were less turbulent. The type of "organized democracy," where interest organizations are included in national policy making, provided a means of incorporating separate views into the decision-making process. And although we associate contemporary Scandinavia with "affluence for all," the collective experience of Scandinavians in the nineteenth century was one of economic hardship. It was so difficult to make a living that many Scandinavians traveled by sea to North America in search of a better life. When common institutions and success in global markets permitted an unforeseen level of economic security in the postwar period, members of these societies retained a shared ambivalence to privately accumulated wealth.

RURAL VALUES

Scandinavians are guided by unwritten social codes that evolved from rural living. The norms of "solidarity" and "egalitarianism" can be traced to how people interacted in the countryside and are documented in literature and anthropology. According to Swedish author Vilhelm Moberg, the origins of Scandinavian values developed from a thousand-year tradition of living in small villages. "The most positive aspect of the village community was its unwritten laws for mutual aid and assistance. Here their fellowship was without flaw. People behaved above all helpfully toward one another, as if it were the most natural thing in the world. 'You help me, and tomorrow I'll help you,' was the rule."[3]

Danish author Aksel Sandemose codified the egalitarian rules of interaction his "law of Jante" or *janteloven* in his classic work *A Fugitive Crosses His Tracks* (1936). Jante is an imaginary village where a young boy encounters his elders and develops an understanding of the social code. Among other things, the ten laws of Jante say: "You should not think you are better than anyone else," and "Do not try to teach us anything." They are intended to equalize members of society or "hold the pack in check."[4] Sandemose's analysis of egalitarianism was deliberately critical and remains a source of debate in Scandinavia today.[5]

The artifacts in Scandinavian homes celebrate the connections of members of these societies to their agrarian past. Wooden utensils, painted chests, and depictions in Scandinavian art of peasant homes and rural settings are the most valuable antiques in modern Scandinavia. Most Scandinavians retain a second home, typically in the countryside or close to the sea. Connections to the periphery and the farm endure, despite the increasing attractiveness of urban life. As wealthy Scandinavians build more ostentatious summer homes, the critical reactions expressed by members of these societies in the media reflect the simplicity and egalitarianism of an earlier era.

Other cultural influences have reinforced an "ideology of social partnership," one of the three defining features of the seven small European states described by Peter Katzenstein (1985). In particular, the role of the church and religious movements in Scandinavia influenced how these societies have developed to the present day.

RELIGION AND SOCIETY

Scandinavia experienced the unifying cultural effects of belonging to one religious community. The establishment of a national religion in each state's constitution has structured the relationship between the citizen and the state. As religious scholar Ole Riis puts it,

> When one religious community has a near monopoly, such as the Scandinavian ones, that church may therefore be a legal platform for expressing

the we-feeling of all inhabitants. In societies where several churches operate alongside each other, they can only appeal to some vague common denominator, when they are to express the sense of solidarity in the whole, complex society.[6]

In Finland and Iceland, the church monopoly influence was somewhat weaker than in Sweden, Norway, or Denmark. However, throughout Scandinavia religious uniformity was strictly enforced, requiring all inhabitants to abide by Lutheranism. Thus, in Scandinavia, nationality and membership in the Lutheran Church are intertwined.

During the medieval period, Scandinavia adhered to the dominant world-view, Roman Catholicism. However, after the Reformation, Scandinavia gradually adopted the Protestant faith, requiring citizens to support and participate in the state church. But, by the eighteenth and nineteenth centuries, Protestant revivalism spread throughout northern Europe—challenging the hierarchy of state churches. The Christian lay movement took hold throughout the rural areas. These organizations established independent prayer houses portrayed as more spiritual than the official churches. Religious dissent was tolerated—until members of the lay church movement violated the law. The dissenters were more numerous in Norway than elsewhere in Scandinavia. The most famous example was the movement led by Hans Nielsen Hauge, a farmer and lay preacher who was imprisoned in Norway in 1804.

The religious movement outside the official church had widespread social consequences for these societies. "Bibles were distributed, and the Bible became the reading of the people as never before; indeed for many it was, till about the middle of the century, practically their only reading matter, greatly enriching not only the religious but the whole intellectual life of the people. It was an oft-quoted saying that the 'Bible and the Constitution' expressed the spirit of the peasant homes."[7]

The religious revivalist movement also established international missionary societies. These groups published newspapers and periodicals with images of foreign lands and provided a channel for international activism just as Scandinavia began establishing its own domestic mechanisms for alleviating poverty.[8] Both Sweden and Norway established missionary societies in the late 1800s, where women played a critical role in organizing church activities.

Missionaries and church leaders provide early examples of international activism. For the missionary societies, there was both an "inner mission" (work at home) and an "outer mission" (work abroad). With respect to the outer mission, Scandinavians were active long before their governments adopted a commitment overseas. For example, Norwegian-born missionary Niels Otto Tank (1800–1864) sought to free the slaves in Surinam. His efforts were justified by moral and ethical considerations. A prominent Swedish bishop,

Knut Henning Gezelius von Scheele, visited Palestine in 1898 and established the Swedish Society for Jerusalem. In subsequent years, the Swedes founded a school and a hospital in Bethlehem. The bishop of Oslo, Eivind Berggrav, joined a team of Scandinavians in the pursuit of peace during the first year of World War II. Berggrav was a well-known public figure with contacts in both the ecumenical movement and the Oxford movement (two international efforts to promote peace).[9]

Prior to the signing of the Universal Declaration of Human Rights (1948), prominent Scandinavian church leaders and religious organizations promoted the rights of the individual.[10] And the role of religion in society promoted an ideology of social justice, egalitarianism, and a moral obligation to alleviate poverty that preceded the adoption of the welfare state. In the postwar period, Scandinavian governments and nongovernmental organizations (NGOs) (the Red Cross and People's Aid Societies) took up the cause of providing overseas assistance initiated by international missionaries.[11]

The church and its leaders have been as important in defining the social order and political institutions as another movement that directly countered its beliefs. The working-class movement opposed the church and offered a separate set of beliefs and principles about the nature of society. The twentieth-century commitment to a united, universal welfare state is a compromise between the Marxist principles of the labor movement and the worldview of the Protestant church. For example, Tim Knudsen traces how a prominent Danish bishop named Martensen published a book entitled *Socialism and Christianity* (1874), which outlined ways to counter the free market and alleviate the problems of the working class by establishing health care, pensions, and unemployment insurance.[12] Thus, the role of religion in society contributed to the adoption of a Protestant worldview, articulated in the domestic and foreign-policy–making agendas of these societies.

In Scandinavian politics and society today, the remnants of the old religious movements are still visible. Each of the five parliaments includes small or medium-sized parties with religious affiliation—from the Christian League in Finland to the Christian People's Party in Denmark and Norway to Christian Democrats in Sweden to the Christian Movement in Iceland.[13] And even though church attendance has declined throughout Scandinavia, the legacy of a unified religious community remains a prominent dimension of the culture and politics of these societies.

Christian organizations call for debt relief between north and south and promote issues of social justice. Pastors and bishops openly criticize the direction and substance of government policies in the Scandinavian media and are part of the cultural debate over the direction of these societies. Most importantly, Scandinavian ministries and foreign-policy makers have adopted agendas once the priority of church organizations and missionaries. As stated by the Norwegian minister of international development Hilde F. Johnson in a speech to the parliament in 2002, "Fifty years ago, in this chamber, NOK [Norwegian kroner] 10 million was allocated to the Aid Fund for Underdeveloped Countries. It was not, perhaps, a large sum, even for those days. But it was still a radical decision for a country that had just emerged from a war, and that was itself receiving assistance."[14]

Scandinavia has shared another cultural experience—its dependence on natural resources.

NATURAL RESOURCE DEPENDENCE

Scandinavia made the transition from economic backwardness to affluence by processing natural resources and exporting finished and semi-finished products to foreign markets. Finland relied on timber and paper; Iceland and Norway depended on the resources of the sea, international shipping, and small agricultural holdings; Sweden relied on mining, timber, and agriculture; and Denmark depended on the farming sector for its economic prosperity. By establishing national authority over these economic assets, Scandinavians retained ownership and direction over how vital sectors developed.

As these societies modernized, governments cooperated with representatives from industry to guide economic development. In Denmark, agricultural cooperatives developed, which enabled vital improvements in production and export promotion. In Finland, close regulation of the timber industry secured these resources for future generations. When Norway began producing energy from its waterfalls, a national concession system was established to restrict foreign ownership, which later became a model for regulating the national petroleum industry. The economic model of development practiced in Scandinavia is referred to as "growth through equity," and depended on "a high standard of education, a high degree of cooperative organization among farmers and the emerging working class, stable democratic structural conditions and a moderate degree of intervention by the state, which promoted social progress without dictating an authoritarian model of development."[15]

Another shared influence defines Scandinavian societies. Ever since the Viking Age, a system of conflict mediation enabled feuding members of society to negotiate settlements based on commonly agreed upon rules. During the era of nation building and constitution writing (1814–1945), legal systems were adopted that specified the relationship between the individual and the state.

LAW AND SOCIETY

Constitutions in Scandinavia are the highest form of legal authority, guiding parliamentary activity and establishing parameters for the individual's relationship to the state. In Scandinavia, the constitution-making process was influenced by political developments inside and outside the region—particularly in North America and elsewhere in Europe. Whereas some societies rely on systems of common law, Scandinavians strictly adhere to principles adopted in their national constitutions. Sociologists consider Scandinavians to be among the most law-abiding citizens in the world—even though, in practice, according to a prominent Norwegian observer, tax evasion is a national pastime.

Following the period of absolutism, constitution makers prioritized the power of the people to determine their own destiny (popular sovereignty). To prevent abuse of central authority, members of these societies adopted a system of separation of powers. The freedoms and rights codified in the American and French constitutions were influential in guiding the process of constitution writing in Scandinavia. Even though Scandinavians did not establish a separate bill of rights, clauses were specifically adopted to protect fundamental principles of human rights.

Scandinavian constitutions share three features: popular sovereignty (the power of the people); separation of powers among several branches of government; and the protection of individual rights. National legislatures are designated to represent and protect the interests of the individual; and consistent with other democracies, power has been delineated among the executive, legislative and judicial branches of government. Some oversight among the different branches is required—inspired by the American system. The most dynamic aspect of the Scandinavian constitutions is the designation of rights—which have evolved from restrictive to expansive.

Individual freedoms and rights are either formally included in national constitutions, or, as in Norway, political and judicial authorities have interpreted their constitution liberally. Freedom of expression and the freedom of association and assembly are guaranteed, enabling broad participation in the political process.

Under Scandinavian law, individuals are protected from excessive state intervention. In some national constitutions, the rights of the individual are more strictly outlined than in others. The Finnish constitution, for example, has fewer limitations on state intervention in society. Civil liberties are protected under the constitution, forbidding the state to deprive individuals of their freedom without legal process.[16] If property is expropriated by the state, individuals are entitled to receive appropriate compensation.

In recent decades, Scandinavian constitutions have been modified to reflect changes in society. As the state's authority expanded, another mechanism was adopted to give individuals a means of protecting themselves from bureaucratic authorities. The office of the ombudsman (elected by the parliament) was created to handle complaints about unfair treatment of citizens.

In addition, the rights of the individual have been expanded to include the freedom of religion. Originally, the Scandinavian constitutions designated one faith and required citizens and government leaders to belong to the church. As stated in the Norwegian Constitution of 1814, "The Evangelical-Lutheran Religion shall be maintained and constitute the established Church of the Kingdom. The inhabitants who profess the said religion are bound to educate their children in the same. . . . In the offices of the state must only be employed those citizens who profess the Evangelical-Lutheran religion."[17]

In recent decades, the right to run for office and vote in local elections has been expanded to include those who have lived in the state for at least three years. Constitutions also designate particular social rights to be provided by the state—from the right to a free education to the provision of support for those unable to take care of themselves.[18]

Scandinavians have based their foreign policies on the same sets of assumptions operational at home. Human rights and freedoms are to be protected, based on mutually accepted principles. Just as these citizens abide by a contract between the citizen and the state, Scandinavian foreign-policy makers pursue protections based on international legal agreements or treaties. Prominent individuals from these societies have enabled Scandinavia to maintain a stellar international reputation—even in difficult times.

According to Andrew Hurrell, international norms "do not develop as a result of direct interplay of state interests or because of the functional benefits which they provide. Rather, they depend on a common moral awareness in the thoughts of individuals."[19] The following analysis connects the strengthening of international norms to a particular site and set of actors.

PROMINENT SCANDINAVIANS

In the twentieth century, a group of prominent Scandinavians played a leading role in establishing a reputation for these societies in world politics. By rejecting the status quo and asking more of existing institutions, these individuals left a legacy that continues to inspire others. In addition to the enduring legacy of Alfred Nobel (1833–1896), who established the highest form of recognition in international society for efforts to promote conflict resolution, Scandinavia's role as a norm entrepreneur has been strengthened by the ideas and careers of Raoul Wallenberg, Dag Hammarskjold, and Olof Palme of Sweden; Christian X, Uffe Ellemann-Jensen, and Svend Auken of Denmark; Fridtjof Nansen, Johan Castberg, and Johan Jorgen Holst of Norway; Uhro Kekkonen and Martti Ahtisaari of Finland; and Vigdis Finnbogadottir of Iceland. Each of the Swedish leaders lost their lives as public servants for international causes, and, as a consequence, their legacies are almost mythical.

The Swedish diplomat Raoul Wallenberg (1912–??) was responsible for rescuing thousands of Hungarian Jews from Nazi persecution at the close of World War II. Acting independently from government authorities, Wallenberg issued Swedish passports from his diplomat post in Budapest. The passports were accepted by German authorities and saved the recipients from arrest and detention. Wallenberg was imprisoned by Russian troops in 1945 and the remainder of his life remains a mystery. Recent information released by Russian authorities suggests that he was shot in Moscow at the headquarters of the Soviet secret police. Wallenberg's efforts are widely known and internationally commemorated. He, along with other prominent Swedes, is associated with humanitarian intervention.

Dag Hammarskjold (1905–1961) served as secretary-general of the UN during the height of the Cold War (1953–1961). Formerly a member of the Swedish Foreign Service, Hammarskjold took his role as international civil servant very seriously and sought to strengthen the capacity of the UN. Raised in a family committed to public and civil service (his father, Hjalmar, was prime minister of Sweden during World War I), Hammarskjold is credited with revitalizing and enhancing the UN.

Hammarsjkold's leadership was important during the negotiation of an international cease-fire following the 1956 Suez crisis. For the first time, a UN Emergency Force intervened to dissipate conflict between states.[20] Hammarskjold is remembered today as strictly upholding the charter of the UN, enhancing the role of secretary-general, and working to resolve international conflict. Many questions remain unanswered regarding Hammarskjold's unexpected death in 1961. He was on a peace mission in southern Africa and died in a plane crash. His strong objections to the rule of Congo president Moise Tshombe have led to numerous conspiracy theories.[21] Visitors to the UN headquarters in New York City will pass by Dag Hammarskjold Plaza, an example of the enduring memory of an international Swedish civil servant.

Olof Palme (1927–1986) became an internationally known advocate for the underclass in world politics. He was widely recognized for his bold views—including sharp criticism of America's war in Vietnam and support for southern African liberation movements. Palme served as the prime minister of Sweden and was committed to promoting Third World development as a member of the international socialist movement. In 1982, Palme assembled a distinguished team of international leaders to create the Commission for Disarmament and Security, known as the Palme Commission. Ironically, under Palme's leadership, the Swedes negotiated an important arms deal ($1.3 billion) for the national gun manufacturer, Bofors, with the Indian military. The controversy surrounding the arms deal was never fully resolved when Palme was assassinated in 1986. However, Palme's legacy has been enhanced by members of his party, the Social Democrats, who have "turned him into something of a saintly figure."[22] As described in the memoirs of Social Democrat Pierri Schiori, under Palme's leadership there were numerous instances of international efforts to promote conflict resolution and social justice—including initiatives to establish contact between Henry Kissinger and the Angola government in the 1970s.

The Danes earned widespread admiration in international society for collective, spontaneous action to protect Jewish citizens from persecution by the Nazis during World War II. Instead of reporting their whereabouts to German authorities during the occupation of Denmark, an underground movement with cooperation from other sectors of society launched an impressive rescue operation. Nearly every Danish Jew made it safely across the water to Sweden.

Denmark's King Christian X became a mythical figure during World War II. When the Nazis required all Jewish citizens to wear the Star of David, Christian X reportedly wore one on his suit during his ritual of riding through the streets of Copenhagen. In recent years, historians have revealed this story to be more legendary than factual.[23] Nonetheless, the international and self-recognition of Danes as an "enlightened and tolerant people" who viewed their Jewish minority as "Danish" only becomes challenged decades after the events, in an age of multiculturalism.[24]

Uffe Ellemann-Jensen, former foreign minister, member of the Danish Parliament and chairman of the Liberal Party, was widely respected for his role in European politics and his leadership during the transformation of East-West relations. Ellemann-Jensen worked to stabilize the newly independent Baltic States (Estonia, Latvia, and Lithuania), and the Danes were first to establish an official presence in the Baltics following their independence. He advocated extending EU membership to Central and Eastern European states and endorsed the efforts of European states to create a common defense—even though this was controversial at home.[25] Although Danes have played a controversial role in the European integration process, Ullemann-Jensen earned a reputation as a multilateralist and was a finalist for the position of secretary-general of the North Alantic Treaty Organization (NATO) during the mid-1990s.

In the 1970s, the Scandinavians led the international community in creating cabinet-level positions for environmental activists. Numerous measures have since been adopted, and Denmark has earned international visibility for its innovative policies. Svend Auken, minister of environment and energy, has taken measures to enhance Denmark's green image in world politics. In 2001, under Auken's leadership, Denmark became the first nation in the world to ban lead. By establishing goals for reducing lead consumption and proposing lead substitutes, the Danes have attracted international attention. The ministry has also been a platform for other environmental initiatives—including changes in the agricultural sector and measures to implement the Kyoto Protocol on reducing carbon emissions.

Norwegian polar explorer and diplomat Fridtjof Nansen (1861–1930) was a national hero, recognized for his work in Russia in the 1920s to prevent hunger and assist refugees. In a country where achievement in sports has been so critical to the development of the nation, Nansen's excellence in skiing was widely praised and became an asset in his polar expeditions. Nansen served as Norway's first representative to the League of Nations and gained widespread international support for the repatriation of prisoners and those displaced by war through the creation of "Nansen passports." Nansen severely criticized Mussolini's occupation of Corfu and gathered support from other national leaders to call for Italy's withdrawal. Even though the League of Nations failed to achieve the aims anticipated by its founders, it became a precursor for postwar international collaboration and institution building. Nansen demonstrated how small states exert a moral authority on larger powers: "The Scandinavian contribution . . . has been to serve as an ever-alert conscience to the Great Powers."[26] Nansen's former home just outside Oslo is now the site of an international research institute, the Fridtjof Nansen Institute (FNI), that promotes greater understanding of international development, peace and conflict resolution, and global resource management.

Scandinavians attracted international attention for constructing humanitarian institutions in domestic society. While Gunnar and Alva Myrdal became the focus of international attention in Sweden for their role in policy entrepreneurship, a leading politician named Johan Castberg (1909–1915) worked to expand social policies in Norway. As a member of parliament, Castberg initiated numerous measures to assist workers in buying homes, increased contributions for those without jobs, and provided sickness insurance policies designed to "place Norway in the forefront of social reform."[27] Castberg also worked to establish a separate social affairs department and as its first leader, advanced greater protections for workers, children, and the unemployed.[28]

Former Norwegian foreign and defense minister Johan Jorgen Holst was educated at Columbia University in international relations and served in the cabinet of Social Democratic prime minister Gro Harlem Brundtland. Holst promoted multilateral diplomacy, positioned Norway to serve as the conscience of larger powers, and became one of the brokers of peace in the Middle East. During the 1980s and early 1990s, Holst brought international attention to the foreign and security policy concerns facing Norway. He also supported Brundtland's refusal to comply with the international ban on commercial whaling by defending the activity as "sustainable." When a group of Palestine Liberation Organization (PLO) and Israeli leaders met at a small farmhouse outside of Oslo, Holst was a key figure in drafting the Oslo Accord. Since his tragic death, other Norwegians, such as Jan Egeland, have initiated international peacekeeping efforts inspired by the Oslo process.

Finns are perceived as "the little country that stood up to the Russians." The capacity to export products to both East and West and retain amicable relations with both blocs during the Cold War depended on shrewd diplomacy. During the height of the Cold War (1961–1963), President Uhro Kekkonen was confronted with a diplomatic crisis. The Soviet Union sent a note to the Finnish government requesting direct military consultations in October of 1961. Finland's treaty of 1948 required the government to come to the assistance of the Soviet Union—a unique arrangement in the Scandinavian area and a legacy of Finland's military cooperation with Germany during World War II. Finnish leaders sought to dissipate the conflict and protect the integrity of Finland's policy of neutrality. Kekkonen adopted two strategies during the crisis. He focused on the nonmilitary aspects of the note, and he met personally with Khrushchev in Novosibirsk, where a mutual understanding was reached and the military consultations were deferred.[29] Kekkonen served as the president of Finland for twenty-five years and is associated with cultivating neighborly relations with the Soviet Union, preserving Finland's neutrality, enabling Finland to play a role in UN peacekeeping efforts, and encouraging international leaders to hold conferences in Finland's capital, Helsinki.[30]

With the end of the Cold War, Finland has made dramatic changes in its foreign relations—from entering the EU on January 1, 1995, to cooperating with NATO. Martti Ahtisaari, formerly with the UN and the Finnish diplomatic service, was elected the tenth president of Finland in 1994. He played a key role in the Balkan conflict, negotiating the terms of the Kosovo settlement between the Americans and Russians. Ahtisaari has also advocated a series of innovative policies to assist the region. In requesting international support to establish programs for youth and children "to develop the skills and values they need to participate in society rather than be excluded from it," Ahtisaari called on leaders to "find ways to go beyond our accustomed thinking, and perhaps even outside our institutional constraints and structures to find innovative ways to strengthen, expand and build upon the excellent work already being done."[31]

When Finland served its rotation in the EU presidency, Ahtisaari engaged in a classic form of small-state critical diplomacy. Relying on the backing of regional partners, Ahtisaari condemned Russia's use of excessive force in Chechnya. In his words, "We urge Russia to observe its commitment to international law . . . we strongly underline the need of dialogue between the Russian government and the elected leaders of the northern Caucuses, including Chechnya."[32] In another forum, Ahtisaari pursued closer integration between Russia and the EU, through introduction of the Northern Dimension initiative. The initiative, led by the Finns, has encouraged closer cooperation between Russia and the EU on a broad range of issues—from energy to environmental protection to trade in raw materials. Finland's geopolitical position and historic relations with Russia have enhanced its capacity to play a distinct role in the aftermath of the Cold War.

Following the tragic events of September 11, 2001, Ahtisaari reinforced the importance of effective international cooperation to resolve the collective global security threats confronting international society. "Many of the most serious threats to security today are global. In addition to terrorism, there is corruption, organized crime, drug trafficking, and the proliferation of small weapons."[33] European-Atlantic political cooperation is more important now than ever in Ahtisaari's assessment.

The least visible of the Scandinavians in world politics are the Icelanders. When NATO established a base on Icelandic territory after World War II, this led to widespread discontent. Icelanders developed a fierce reputation against British fishing fleets during the Cod Wars (see details in chapter 5). And Icelanders have been the most resistant to European integration, as they seek to protect vital natural resources. Multilateral forms of cooperation are less attractive to the residents of this island in the north. Even though Iceland advocates global governance, the Icelanders have sought other means of building an international reputation.

In 1980, Iceland attracted international attention as the first parliamentary democracy to elect a female president. Vigdis Finnbogadottir was a well-known cultural figure in Icelandic society and became a well-respected politician. She was a founding member of the Save the Children Association and among the first single women in Iceland to adopt a child. During the Cold War, Iceland was strategically important because of its geopolitical position. Consistent with the Scandinavian practice of bridge building between the great powers, the government of Iceland hosted the historic meeting between U.S. President Ronald Reagan and Soviet leader Mikhail Gorbachev in the 1980s. Finnbogadottir has remained internationally active and is well respected for her leadership role(s) in Iceland and as a member and chair of the Council of Women World Leaders at Harvard's John F. Kennedy School.

As seen from abroad, Scandinavians have quietly and consistently articulated a particular view of how we should live, the ways in which power should be exercised, and the obligations of states and international authorities to uphold and respect basic rights and freedoms. While the preceding analysis focuses on the most highly acclaimed Scandinavians, many of the efforts of norm entrepreneurship are less visible and are part of the everyday activities of an international group of civil servants. For example, Swedish diplomats authored a declaration in the UN that became the basis for the General Assembly's "Declaration on the Protection of All Persons from Being Subjected to Torture or Other Cruel, Inhuman or Degrading Treatment or Punishment."[34] The Convention against Torture was formally adopted by the United Nations in 1984.

The extent of Scandinavia's role is not limited to political leaders. Members of Scandinavia's literary community have also exported values and pushed for innovations at home and abroad. Early criticisms of societal rigidities and inequalities emanated from the works of nineteenth-century Norwegian writers Henrik Ibsen, Camilla Collett, and Amalie Skram. Danish author Hans Christian Andersen (1805–1875) is best known for his fairy tales and stories written for children. However, "Andersen was acutely aware of the inequities of Danish society, having experienced most of them first-hand, and throughout his works, he expresses sympathy for the poor and scorn for the pompous."[35] During the mid-1800s, Fredrika Bremer criticized the social conditions facing single women in Sweden. In the twentieth century, Swedish author Astrid Lindgren depicted social values in her books for children and became an international advocate for animal rights. These are only a few examples of the depth of international reputation building outside the foreign policy arena.

SCANDINAVIA AND GLOBAL SOCIETY

What kind of international society are Scandinavia and Scandinavians seeking to create? By examining the documents produced by these governments, the Nordic Council (a nongovernmental cooperative forum) and national research institutes, there is a clear pattern in the issues/areas where Scandinavians devote time, energy, and resources in world politics. Documents produced by Scandinavian foreign policy makers are an indicator of how these societies seek to play a role. Since 1945, five thematic areas have been emphasized—from conflict prevention, human rights, egalitarianism, and poverty assistance to promoting sustainable development.

A speech by Swedish foreign minister Anna Lindh made in September 1999 expresses a Scandinavian view of conflict prevention:

> Enormous human and economic costs are involved in violent conflicts, costs that citizens and taxpayers are no longer prepared to bear. It is not only a humanitarian imperative but also in our own interest to use human and economic resources for prevention and building a better common future rather than destroying conditions for development. We need a global culture of conflict prevention.[36]

In this spirit, the Swedes have developed an action plan for early intervention in conflict situations. The five main goals outlined by the Swedish foreign ministry are promoting a culture of prevention; identifying structural risk factors; developing the international system of norms and strengthening its implementation; strengthening the international institutional framework and its preventive instruments; and strengthening the capacity in Sweden for international conflict prevention in different policy areas.[37]

Through a diversity of channels, Scandinavians advocate strengthening measures to protect human rights. According to the official documents, "measures to advance human rights are an important instrument of Norwegian foreign policy."[38] Norwegian authorities have negotiated numerous agreements and partnered with like-minded states to create frameworks for strengthening international cooperation in human rights. By working with NGOs and developing new measures to protect the individual, Norwegians (often in partnership with other Scandinavians) are norm entrepreneurs in the field of human rights.

International efforts to promote equality are also priorities for Scandinavian foreign policy makers. In 1974, the Nordic Council of Ministers initiated a cooperative program to promote equal opportunities for women throughout Scandinavia. In 2001, the Nordic Council created a working group to develop measures to halt trafficking of women. As Pierre Schiori, Swedish minister for international development and cooperation, stated, "Democracy, human rights, poverty—how can work on these fields be considered perfectly satisfactory if half of humanity is ignored?"[39]

Assistance for development in the Baltic area has been a central element of Scandinavian foreign-policy making during the 1990s. Each of the Scandinavian governments has reached out to assist individual Baltic States— Iceland gave early recognition of independence; Sweden made efforts to clean up the Baltic Sea; Finland helped train Estonian defense forces; and Norway and Denmark had roles in promoting education. Collectively, Scandinavian governments have also provided assistance as members of the Nordic Council. In 1991, the ministerial council allocated two million Danish crowns

($325,000) to enable Baltic participation in human rights conferences, provide training for journalists, offer environmental education for teachers, and present a seminar on government financing for economists.[40] As Swedish Conservative Party leader Carl Bildt has argued, securing the stability of the Baltic area is an important step in eventually bringing Russia into closer cooperation with Western institutions.

The Scandinavians have also exercised leadership in international environmental policy making. Measures adopted by the UN documented in the report *Our Common Future* and defined as "sustainable development" are strongly endorsed by governments and foreign-policy makers.

The UN's Brundtland Commission (led by Norwegian Gro Harlem Brundtland) defined sustainable development as international cooperation to incorporate ecological criteria into economic growth plans, as part of a long-term strategy to ensure the wealth-creating possibilities of future generations. Since the report was published, Scandinavians have been active in its implemention—from participation in global environmental conferences to national measures designed to meet internationally agreed-upon criteria for sustainability. For example, in the report "Working towards Sustainable Development," the following goal is laid out: "The Government's ambition is for Sweden to be an international leader and model country in the creation of a sustainable society."[41]

The Swedish government also introduced new measures for ecological sustainability to the parliament in 1998, "Sustainable Sweden—Progress Report and New Measures for an Ecologically Sustainable Development." Included among the numerous initiatives to improve the environment are: Sweden's active participation in a Global Environmental Fund for co-financing projects in the developing world; support for the inclusion of environmental considerations in the World Trade Organization (WTO); and active participation in global conventions pertaining to sustainable development. Corporate images produced by the Scandinavian Airlines System and IKEA reproduce national images of ecological responsibility and reinforce public perceptions of these societies in the international community.

Oran Young demonstrates how Scandinavians have set the international agenda in global environmental policy making. The Finns were a critical player in establishing the Arctic Environmental Protection Strategy (AEPS), a new cooperative regime in northern Europe. By seizing an opportunity to link Russia to the West, Finnish policy makers brought to the table a group of states committed to improving socioeconomic conditions in the Arctic area. "Finland emerged as the driving force behind the effort to place environmental protection in the Arctic on the international political agenda during 1988. The Finns not only started the ball rolling but also refused to let the

issue fade away in the face of disinterest on the part of many and actual an-
tagonism on the part of some."[42] According to Oran Young, Finnish motives
were not merely altruistic but also advanced the interests of the Finnish state
and society. Thus, building an international reputation as norm entrepreneurs
is not only how the Scandinavians define themselves as global good citizens;
it may also serve the interests of a group of societies that depend on the world
economy and the stability of the region for their prosperity and survival.

In recent decades, scholars and observers have documented the decline
of the Scandinavian way of life—from the decreasing support for the Social
Democratic party to the growing power of business in national decision making to the conventional levels of unemployment more typical of other European states to the reduction in social welfare benefits, the influx of non-
Scandinavians, and the exodus of flagship companies abroad. Because of the
long-standing commitment at home to principles of human rights, equality,
social justice, and environmentalism, Scandinavians have had an unrivaled legitimacy in promoting higher standards for the international community.
However, these societies are undergoing new challenges, and many observers
are reassessing their perceptions of Scandinavian systems. How have Scandinavian society and politics changed, and to what extent have these changes affected their reputation(s) and capacity to exercise influence in structuring the
international agenda in world politics?

POLITICAL CHANGE AND GLOBAL AGENDA SETTING

Since the 1960s, Scandinavia has experienced political and social changes that
have brought into question the capacity of these societies to retain a distinctive way of life. Demographically, the populations of northern Europe are becoming less homogeneous as more and more immigrants migrate to Scandinavia. In addition, the populations of these societies are aging—making it
more expensive to provide health-care and welfare services. More members of
these societies are unemployed, which also raises costs to the state. And as
Scandinavia's largest recipient of exports (the European Community, or EC)
unifies, this poses a challenge for political leaders. The end of the Cold War
created new security vulnerabilities in the north, and corresponded with an
economic downturn in eastern Scandinavia (particularly in Finland). European integration became one of the most divisive foreign policy questions in
Scandinavia. Some states opted to join the EC (Denmark in 1973; Sweden
and Finland in 1995), while others remain more loosely engaged (Norway
and Iceland).

There are notable transformations in how social power is exercised in Scandinavia today. Domestic institutions have had difficulty absorbing immigrant labor, and these groups have been less successful in gaining a voice in Scandinavian politics. Immigrant groups remain divided and have yet to be cultivated by the major political parties.[43] Highly publicized incidents of intolerance and xenophobia undermine the solidarity of Scandinavian societies and expose new cleavages in these societies. Some indicators of social inclusion are promising—such as favorable reception of contemporary films documenting differences and the multiplicity of ethnic restaurants throughout Scandinavia that have diversified the cultural options there. Thus, the underlying values of equality and justice are being tested as Scandinavia seeks to integrate new groups into the social fabric.

The end of the Cold War has focused attention on what goes on within states—not just on the prospect of conflict between states. Since the 1990s, the role of norms has become a more visible aspect of international politics. Transnational social movements led to the end of the system of apartheid in South Africa; international protesters disrupt meetings of the WTO; human rights considerations are the basis for intervention in the former Yugoslavia; and environmentalists clash over the appropriate means of managing the global commons. In this transformation of global priorities, Scandinavia's reputation, identity, and interests are a good fit with changes in the international system.

Scandinavia's image as ecological societies remains unrivaled. In global ratings of sustainability, Scandinavia heads the list for maintaining favorable environmental conditions.[44] And Scandinavian leaders have retained (and in some cases, enhanced) their capacity to act as international negotiators and promoters of conflict resolution. Aid policy remains generous, consistent with the retention of a national commitment to universal social welfare. Despite the reported decline of Scandinavian solidarity in domestic politics, commitments to international agendas are remarkably resilient in foreign-policy making.

In response to more competitive world markets and the elimination of the classic threats to national security associated with the Cold War, Scandinavian governments have deepened cooperation with European partners. However, the five states of northern Europe are divided between those who are full participants in the European integration process and those who remain more aloof. Denmark has been a member the longest (since 1973), yet has continually resisted the transfer of power away from Copenhagen. Denmark, along with Sweden and Finland, acts within the formal institutions of European governance, whereas Norway and Iceland have the capacity to pursue global agenda setting outside the formal channels of EU cooperation.

As Scandinavian governments face transformations in society and international politics, how has their capacity for international agenda setting been influenced? Some transformations at home (especially the influx of ethnic minorities) make it more problematic for Scandinavia to act as a moral superpower. It is difficult to advocate higher standards abroad when there are divisions at home. Yet in other areas, the transformations in the world provide new opportunities for Scandinavia to exercise influence by exporting ideas that emanate from long-standing commitments to human rights, justice, solidarity, equality, and resource management. When UN secretary-general Kofi Annan establishes special commissions to investigate humanitarian conditions or explore possibilities for conflict resolution, prominent Scandinavians (such as Thorvald Stoltenberg, Jan Egeland, and Martti Ahtisaari) are leading candidates.

However, all of Scandinavia is not equally capable of playing a global role in the twenty-first century. For some states (Sweden and Finland), the capacity to act alone has been weakened because of a legal commitment by treaty to abide by the common policies negotiated in Brussels. The necessity of cooperating with Europe has changed the priorities of the foreign policy establishment. This is particularly apparent in Sweden.[45] As the following chapter demonstrates, Swedish and Finnish foreign-policy making seeks to reform the EU from within. And even though these societies are required to accept European decisions, they have proven that "being at the table" can bring about changes in the direction and substance of European cooperation.

NOTES

1. See Peter Esaiasson and Knut Heidar (eds.), *Beyond Westminster and Congress: The Nordic Experience* (Columbus: Ohio State University Press, 2000), and Olof Petersson, *The Government and Politics of the Nordic Countries* (Stockholm: Fritzes, 1994).

2. See Peter J. Katzenstein, *Small States in World Markets* (Ithaca, NY: Cornell University Press, 1985).

3. Vilhelm Moberg, "Life in the Villages," in *Nordic Views and Values*, edited by Patrik Engellau and Ulf Henning (Stockholm: The Nordic Council, 1984), p. 11.

4. Moberg, "Life in the Villages," p. 29.

5. See Anne Cohen Kiel, *Continuity and Change* (Oslo: Scandinavian University Press, 1993).

6. Ole Riis, "The Role of Religion in Legitimating the Modern Structure of Society," *Acta Sociologica* 32 (1989): 142.

7. Karen Larsen, *A History of Norway* (Princeton, NJ: Princeton University Press, 1950), p. 450.

8. An image of Madagascar (map and sketch) is presented in the 1910 publication *Norsk Misjonstidende* (1910), reprinted in *Kultur Historisk Vegbok* [edited by Nis Georg Brekke (Bergen, Norway: Vestkyst, 1993)] p. 144.

9. Peter W. Ludlow, "Scandinavia between the Great Powers: Attempts at Mediation in the First Year of the Second World War," *Historisk Tidskrift* 1(1974), pp. 6–7.

10. Lennart Molin, "Not for Ourselves Alone," *The Ecumenical Review* 52 (April 2000): 172.

11. For an analysis of how this developed in Norwegian foreign-policy making see Knut Heidar, *Norway: Elites on Trial* (Boulder, CO: Westview Press, 2001), pp. 148–149.

12. Tim Knudsen (ed.), *Den nordiske protestantisme og velfaerdsstaten* (Aarhus, Denmark: Universitetsforlag, 2000), pp. 150–151.

13. Esaiasson and Heidar, *Beyond Westminster and Congress*, pp. 42, 445–453.

14. Norwegian Ministry of Foreign Affairs, "Focus on Norwegian Development Cooperation" (Oslo: Norwegian Ministry of Foreign Affairs, 2002), p. 7.

15. The Nordic Council, *The Source of Liberty: The Nordic Contribution to Europe* (Stockholm: Nordic Council, 1992), p. 193.

16. Petersson, *The Government and Politics of the Nordic Countries*, p. 185.

17. Mads T. Andenaes and Ingeborg Wilberg, *The Constitution of Norway* (Oslo: Universitetsforlaget, 1987), pp. 141, 156.

18. Petersson, *The Government and Politics of the Nordic Countries*, p. 186.

19. Andrew Hurrell, "International Society and the Study of Regimes: A Reflective Approach," in Volker Rittberger, editor, *Regime Theory and International Relations* (Oxford, UK: Clarendon Press, 1993), pp. 65–66.

20. See Dorothy Jones, "The Example of Dag Hammarskjold," *The Christian Century* 111 (November 9, 1994): 1047–1051.

21. David Gibbs, "Dag Hammarskjold, the United Nations and the Congo Crisis of 1960–61: A Reinterpretation," *The Journal of Modern African Studies* 31 (March 1993): 163–175.

22. Pranay B. Gupte and Rahul Singh, "Money! Guns! Corruption!" *Forbes* (July 7, 1997): 112–117.

23. Discussions with Danish expert Marianne Stecher-Hansen, Department of Scandinavian Studies, University of Washington, Seattle, February 12, 2002.

24. See Yael Enoch, "The Intolerance of a Tolerant People: Ethnic Relations in Denmark," *Ethnic and Racial Studies* 17 (April 1994): 282.

25. Interview with Uffe Ellemann-Jensen by Robert Guttmann, in "Danish Business Goes Global," *Europe* 339 (September 1994): 8–10.

26. S. Shepard Jones, *The Scandinavian States and the League of Nations* (Princeton, NJ: Princeton University Press and New York: American Scandinavian Foundation, 1939), p. 274, cited in Larsen, *A History of Norway*, p. 512.

27. Larsen, *A History of Norway*, p. 503.

28. Larsen, *A History of Norway*, pp. 504–505, 525, and discussions with Castberg's relative in Seattle, Brewster Denny.

29. Risto Pentilla, *Finland's Search for Security through Defense, 1944–89* (London: MacMillan, 1991), pp. 100–103.

30. Richard Cavendish, "The Birth of Urho Kekkonen," *History Today* 50 (September 2000): 54.

31. Excerpt from a speech by Martti Ahtisaari, "Future of the Balkans," *Presidents and Prime Ministers* 9 (January 2000): 22.

32. Delegation of the European Commission, "EU Criticizes Russia's Force in Chechnya," *Europe*, December 1999, p. S–3.

33. Interview with *NATO Nytt* (Oslo: Den norske Atlanterhavskomite, Fall 2001), p. 24.

34. Ann Marie Clark, *Diplomacy of Conscience: Amnesty International and Changing Human Rights Norms* (Princeton, NJ: Princeton University Press, 2001), pp. 59–60.

35. Frank Hugus, "Hans Christian Andersen: The Storyteller as Social Critic," *Scandinavian Review* 87 (Autumn 1999): 29.

36. "Create a Worldwide Culture of Conflict Prevention," Swedish Ministry of Foreign Affairs, speeches and articles, September 18, 1999.

37. Swedish Ministry of Foreign Affairs, "Preventing Violent Conflict—A Swedish Action Plan," *UD Info* (May 1999): 1.

38. Norwegian Ministry of Foreign Affairs, "Human Rights 1999: Annual Report on Norwegian Efforts to Promote Human Rights" (Oslo), p. 44.

39. Swedish Ministry for Foreign Affairs, "Gender Equality between Women and Men in Development Co-operation" (Stockholm, 1998), p. 3.

40. Nordic Council of Ministers, "Baltic Projects Get Go-Ahead," *Norden: The Top of Europe*, no. 3 (1991): 1.

41. Regeringskansliet, "Working towards Sustainable Development," The Swedish Ministry of Industry, Employment and Communications, Swedish Government website, 2001, p. 5.

42. Oran Young, *Creating Regimes: Arctic Accords and International Governance* (Ithaca, NY: Cornell University Press, 1998), p. 57.

43. See Jorgen Goul Andersen and Jens Hoff, *Democracy and Citizenship in Scandinavia* (New York: Palgrave, 2001).

44. "Scandinavia Tops World League Table on the Environment," *The Financial Times*, February 2–3, 2002.

45. Hans Mouritzen provides evidence of the abandonment of the Nordic model as an instrument of Swedish foreign-policy making since 1991 in "The Nordic Model as a Foreign Policy Instrument: Its Rise and Fall," *Journal of Peace Research* 32 (1995): 9–21.

· 3 ·

A More Scandinavian EU?

$\mathcal{S}$ince the signing of the Treaty of Rome in 1957, European cooperation has evolved from a loose partnership of six member states to a tight partnership of twenty-five member states. Today, there is a long waiting list for entry, as more and more governments view regional integration as an appropriate means of maintaining competitiveness, ensuring political stability, and securing borders. Since the initial founding of the European Community (EC), the role of France and Germany has been critical to the realization of European-wide cooperation and to the ways in which regional cooperation has evolved.[1] However, larger states are not the only ones with the capacity to set the agenda in European institutions.

The European integration process offers multiple levels for national governments, interest organizations, political parties, and members of industry to organize and voice their preferences. Each member state directly elects members to the European Parliament and appoints representatives to each of the governing bodies of the European Union (EU) (the European Commission, the Council of Ministers, and the European Court of Justice). "The EU can be viewed as an opportunity for small states to participate in a 'society of states' and act multilaterally to achieve common European interests, thereby compensating for their lack of traditional power."[2]

Although Scandinavia entered regional governance relatively late, each of these societies has influenced the integration process—from Denmark's decision to slow the pace of integration symbolized by a citizen's vote against the Maastricht Treaty to European Council agenda setting during the Swedish, Finnish, and Danish EU presidencies. In the absence of a Scandinavian voice, European policy coordination would be less preoccupied with strengthening particular norms—from improving environmental quality, gender equality, and working for more open or transparent decision-making processes to developing innovative means of conflict management and resolution, peacekeeping, and disaster relief operations.[3] This chapter identifies how Scandinavia has sought to influence the substance and direction of EU cooperation, just as the EU has become a more powerful voice in world politics.

EUROPE CONSOLIDATES AUTHORITY

In 1957, the leaders of six European states agreed to create a European Economic Community (EEC) according to principles outlined in the Treaty of Rome. Leading European industrialists and policy makers sought to avoid the tragedies of World Wars I and II by embedding the economies and societies of Europe into an interdependent web. The aims of cooperation were both political and economic. The founders sought to pursue peace through trade. Even though the intentions were consistent with Scandinavian foreign policy priorities, the original six partners (France, Germany, Italy, the Netherlands, Belgium, and Luxembourg) did not include the small northern European states. Instead, Scandinavian governments preferred a less binding form of cooperation created under the leadership of Britain. In 1959, three Scandinavian governments (Sweden, Denmark, and Norway) agreed to participate in the European Free Trade Association (EFTA) by signing bilateral treaties with the EEC.[4] EFTA membership enabled tariff-free trade in industrial goods, yet did not require the transfer of sovereignty to European-wide institutions. Eventually, EFTA membership became attractive to all of Scandinavia. In 1970, Iceland became a member of EFTA, whereas Finland had maintained a special treaty—the Finnish-European Free Trade Agreement (FINEFTA)—with EFTA and became a full member in 1986.

European cooperation has been expanded to include more issues/areas, and its membership has grown to include many more member states since the 1950s, thus becoming deeper and wider in scope. Policy coordination has been significantly expanded from coal and steel trade, agricultural production (the Common Agricultural Policy or "Green Europe"), fisheries (the Common Fisheries Policy or "Blue Europe"), and the creation of a Common Energy Policy to a European-wide monetary policy, common currency, and plans for an integrated military and security policy. Issues once considered the domain of national governments have found a place on the EU's agenda. For example, decisions made by the European-wide Court of Justice in recent decades have served to advance an environmental agenda within the EU. The expanded scope of collective governance is remarkable—given the transfer of authority from the state to the region and the implications for state sovereignty.[5] Table 3.1 indicates some of the ways in which European cooperation has evolved.

Table 3.1. What Has Changed in Europe?

Name Changes
  European Economic Community (EEC)
  European Community (EC)
  European Union (EU)
Important Treaties
  European Coal and Steel Community (ECSC) (1951)
  Treaty of Rome (1957)
  European Free Trade Association (EFTA) (1959)
  Single European Act (SEA) (1985)
  Treaty on European Union (TEU) (1992)
Membership Expansion
  The six original members or "inner six": France, Germany, Italy, Belgium, the
  Netherlands, Luxembourg
  Europe of nine members: original six plus Britain, Denmark, and Ireland
  The twelve member states: original six plus Britain, Denmark, Ireland, Spain, Greece,
  and Portugal
  Expansion includes Slovenia, Poland, Czech Republic, Poland, Hungary, Estonia,
  Latvia, Lithuania, Turkey, Malta, and Cyprus

SCANDINAVIA AND EUROPEAN INTEGRATION

As Europe revitalized its cooperation in the mid-1980s and specified the conditions for an internal market, monetary union, and closer cooperation in defense policy, Scandinavia launched a new debate over the pros and cons of Europeanization.[6]

The collapse of the Soviet empire enabled the Finnish government to contemplate membership in the EU for the first time. The Treaty of Friendship, Cooperation and Mutual Assistance of 1948 established a dependent relationship between Finland and the Soviet Union. This required Finland to come to the assistance of the Soviets in case of an armed attack; called for military consultation in the case of a threat of attack; prohibited entrance by Finland into any alliance against the Soviet Union; and commited each country to respect the other's sovereignty and integrity.[7] The treaty acknowledged Finland's cooperation with Germany in successive military conflicts with Russia during World War II. However, as the bipolar system unraveled, the treaty was declared null and void, and Finland was permitted to enter freely into all forms of international cooperation after 1990.

Across the border in Sweden, the government announced its preference to join the EU—a radical reversal from its previous position to remain aloof from regional cooperation. Sweden, as it turned out, no longer preferred a policy of neutrality and disengagement as markets integrated and industrial leaders pushed for the government to join.

In neighboring Norway, the society engaged in a heated national discussion over whether Europe had more to offer or if the nation-state should remain (again) outside the boundaries of the union. In the fall of 1994, three national referenda were held: first in Finland, where a majority of the voters endorsed European integration; second in Sweden, where a second, less decisive majority approved European integration; and third in Norway, where the anti-EU movement was victorious. Iceland never had enough domestic support during this period to seriously engage the membership question; whereas in Denmark (a member of the EC since 1973), new forms of resistance to the deepening of integration gathered momentum.

With the accession of Sweden and Finland into the EU in 1995, more Scandinavians participate in the institutions, policy making, and agenda setting of regional cooperation. To what extent do Swedes and Finns have a voice in the EU? And how does this differ from the Danes, who have been a part of the regional integration process for decades, yet have rejected recent efforts to deepen cooperation, or from the Norwegians and Icelanders, who want to keep the door open to membership, but do not have the support at home to join? The following discussion identifies the ways in which Scandinavians seek to influence European cooperation.

FROM NEUTRALITY TO PARTNERSHIP

Finland and Sweden initiated a rapid redirection in foreign-policy making in the late 1980s and early 1990s by redefining neutrality policy and actively pursuing membership in the European Union. The unraveling of the Soviet Union revealed how dependent the Finnish economy had been on barter trade with its neighbor. Unemployment soared to 19 percent of the workforce in the early 1990s, and Finns increasingly viewed European integration as the best means of recovery as well as being insurance against new security risks on the lengthy Finnish-Russian border. In a remarkable turnaround, the Finnish government and society became the most pro-European Scandinavians, willingly embracing new regional cooperation. The Finns became the first Scandinavian state to adopt the euro when it was introduced in 2002, and the Finnish government plays an active role in defining how neutral states should contribute to European security and defense arrangements.

Swedish Social Democrats also made an important change of course in the 1980s, accepting regional cooperation as the means of resolving problems at home. Even though many Swedes have reservations about the direction of European cooperation, the official representatives of Swedish government, major industries, and even the trade unionists endorse closer cooperation with Europe as essential for the future health and prosperity of Sweden. Thus, in the European Union, the largest of the Scandinavian states, with the highest international profile, has joined the most important regional trading bloc in the world. And as one prominent Swede put it, "On many occasions, our voice is just one among many. However, when our voice is heard, the consequences are far greater than Sweden acting alone."[8]

How can small states have a voice within EU institutions? One of the five decision-making institutions of the EU is the European Council. As member-states of the EU, Finland, Sweden, and Denmark have each held the presidency of the council for a six-month period. In the position of the presidency, individual member-states set the agenda for the EU. In this capacity, Finland, Sweden, and Denmark have played decisive and distinctive roles. In 1999, Finland prioritized cooperation between the EU and northern Europe (the Northern Dimension). In 2001, Sweden's EU agenda included improving the transparency of EU institutions and promoting higher environmental standards. In 2002, Denmark's EU agenda prioritized enlargement negotiations for ten new member countries and included regional efforts to promote sustainable development, safe food, crime prevention, and global responsibility.

As new constitutional arrangements are adopted to govern an expanded EU, Scandinavia, again, brings a distinctive set of issues to the European institutional reform process.

FINLAND AND THE NORTHERN DIMENSION INITIATIVE

In 1997, Prime Minister Paavo Lipponen made an important speech, calling on the EU to launch a "Northern Dimension" policy. "An active engagement in the Barents region would afford the Union enormous potential to profit from the energy, wood and other natural resources located there. It would also contribute to promoting security in its most northerly border region, as well as reducing the gulf in living standards between the EU and post-communist Russia."[9] The Finns focused the EU's attention on the northernmost corner of Europe where Finland and the EU share a lengthy border with Russia. Some of the measures have been implemented—while others were overshadowed by the war in Chechnya and the difficulty of convincing some members of the EU to cooperate with entities outside the region such as the Arctic Council. However, the Northern Dimension has been incorporated as a part of EU policy since 1998, and as David Arter argues, demonstrates the capacity of small states to exert their influence.[10]

The Finnish government took its role as the agenda setter for the EU very seriously. All ministries devoted their attention to the presidency, and other matters received a lower priority. For a full year prior to assuming the presidency, Finland engaged in preparations for the post. Finland's long-standing relationship with Russia provided legitimacy in seeking new forms of partnership in the north. The launching of the Northern Dimension Initiative is a legacy of Finland's leadership within EU institutions and is a priority of the government in regional cooperation.[11]

At the close of the Finnish presidency, several other agenda items were put forward during the European Council meetings held in Helsinki, December 10–11, 1999. As part of the so-called Millennium Declaration, the council agreed to enhance the transparency and accountability of EU institutions, to seek new forms of security cooperation, to assist societies in the transformation to a knowledge-based economy, to promote human rights, and to pursue sustainable environmental policies. These measures correspond with Finnish foreign-policy–making priorities, and several of these agenda items were incorporated in Sweden's agenda for the EU, January–June, 2001, and Denmark's EU agenda, June 2002–January 2003.

ENLARGEMENT, THE ENVIRONMENT, AND EQUALITY: SWEDEN SETS THE EU AGENDA

The enlargement of the EU to include a new group of member-states became a central issue on Sweden's EU agenda. With twelve states entering into negotiations for entry during the spring of 2001, the Swedish EU presidency (by necessity) focused on the conditions required for the new partners to meet EU criteria for membership. For the Swedes, the agenda for reviewing eligibility for membership included environmental criteria. Swedish trade minister Leif Pagrotsky registered concern about environmental conditions in applicant countries: "Compared to the situation under communism, they are on the path to improvement . . . they are moving, but some of us would like to see that progress going faster."[12]

Since Sweden joined the EU in 1995, one of the ways the government seeks to export its ideas is in the area of environmental policy. As Swedish EU expert Annica Kronsell argues,

> It is notable that Swedish policy makers have had some success in pursuing some of their goals in the area of environmental policy. The EU has adopted an acidification strategy, has agreed to a revision of the chemicals policy and a chemical strategy is in the making. Policy makers also attest

to a whole range of minute successes within a range of negotiations of specific directives.[13]

Even though Swedes are uneasy with being considered a "model" in environmental policy making, they have earned an international reputation in this issue/area, and negotiators bring expertise and knowledge to the EU.[14]

According to Swedish EU representative Anita Gradin, the EU presidency also provided a voice in international politics, as Swedes teamed up with European partners to advocate an agenda—from concern for how America treats its citizens (objections to the death penalty) to raising new priorities for policy makers including trafficking of women.[15] And in partnership with other Scandinavian defense ministries—both inside and outside the EU—Sweden played a critical role in defining (and redefining) the military capacity of the EU.

DENMARK'S EU PRESIDENCY: NORM ENFORCEMENT

The Danish presidency corresponded with the EU's expansion, which brought in ten new member countries. In overseeing the widening of Europe, the Danes implemented the "Copenhagen Criteria," the conditions required for entry into the EU established at the European Council meeting in Copenhagen in 1993. These norms of accession are

> a stable political democracy, protection of minorities and respect for human rights . . . a functioning market economy and economic strength to cope with the competitive pressures with the EU internal market . . . and they must incorporate the EU's comprehensive body of regulations into their national legislation . . . and enforce new laws.[16]

The Danes emphasized the importance of securing accession agreements for the new entrants and pursuing the greatest possible transparency in the process of decision making. The Danish presidency created a home page, eu2002.dk, designed to make information easily accessible and counter perceptions of antidemocratic tendencies in European institutions.

Specific Danish innovations included an EU action plan to combat international terrorism in response to the events of September 11, 2001; collective efforts to combat crime; and effective management of borders and migration. The Danes advocated strengthening the EU's capacity to avert terrorist attacks as part of a common foreign and security policy, extending and improving electronic monitoring of crime (the Schengen Information

System), and more effective integration of third-country nationals into European societies. Danish priorities embodied measures successful at home—from job creation to sustainable energy policies and investment in new technologies.

The Danish agenda advocated EU cooperation with global measures to improve the environment—from encouraging nonmember countries to ratify the Kyoto Protocol to strengthening an EU strategy for sustainable development. Enhanced measures to promote peace and conflict resolution, as well as adherence to UN recommendations for global aid contributions (.7 percent of gross national product) were also part of the Danish agenda—consistent with foreign policy priorities of all Scandinavian governments. These ideas were transmitted to the EU as part of Denmark's 2002 agenda.

PARTNERS FOR PEACE: FINNISH, SWEDISH, AND NORWEGIAN EU COOPERATION

As NATO diversified its tasks and new security risks faced European societies from within the territorial boundaries of states, the northern Europeans initiated a measure to prepare Europe for civil and military threats. As stated by Swedish defense minister Bjorn von Sydow, "The experiences from Kosovo and even Bosnia show the need for a civil component" in European defense planning.[17]

Sweden and Finland successfully launched a joint initiative to incorporate the "Petersberg Tasks" into the Amsterdam Treaty. The Petersberg Tasks refer to humanitarian and rescue efforts, peacekeeping, and crisis management measures and are included in Article 17.2 of the Amsterdam Treaty.

The Finnish and Swedish initiative also received support from the Norwegians, who are associate members of the Western European Union, the EU's cooperative arrangement for defense and security. In July 2000, the Norwegian prime minister Jens Stoltenberg announced the government's intent to support the EU-controlled rapid reaction troops by committing 3,500 Norwegians. As stated by Stoltenberg, "We want to take more global responsibility, and in Europe we want as close a relationship as possible."[18] As Europe develops the European Security and Defense Identity, the Norwegians seek to balance loyalty to NATO with new forms of regional security. According to Defense Minister Eldbjorg Lower, "Our own security is closely bound with that of the EU and its members. The EU is currently engaging in a great deal of activity in the field of security and conflict resolution. Norway wishes to be involved in this work."[19]

Denmark, on the other hand, opposed the Swedish-Finnish initiative and has resisted the expansion of EU competence in the area of security and defense.[20] Consistent with other issues/areas, Danes have tended to view the centralization of authority in the EU critically and have developed a reputation as a society with a strong coalition of citizens skeptical to Europeanization.

RESISTANCE TO CENTRALIZATION: THE DANISH VOICE IN THE EU

Since Denmark became a member of the EC in 1973, societal groups and political parties have voiced reservations about the structure and form of European cooperation. In 1992, the Danes narrowly rejected the Maastricht Treaty. The Danish vote had ripple effects throughout the EU. As one observer put it,

> Danes were treated like heroes for sending a message to the politicians in Brussels that they were out of step with the populations of Europe and going too far towards centralization. By their vote, they forced Europe to make some useful corrections in its political ambitions, which in turn paved the way for Denmark's approval (with certain reservations) of the Maastricht Treaty in 1993.[21]

Danes voted again on September 28, 1999, to determine whether to participate in the European currency unit, the euro. Again, Danes expressed their resistance by voting "no" (53 percent to 47 percent). In the integration process, Danes support the British vision of European unity and have developed a reputation for slowing the speed of European integration. The EU's institutions risk losing legitimacy if Danish (and British) reservations about the course of European cooperation are not addressed in a satisfactory manner.

Another way Danes have influenced the EU is by providing an institutional model to other European states. Denmark was the first state to establish a special parliamentary committee responsible for overseeing EU matters. Other member-states have since adopted an institutional structure similar to the Danes.[22]

As norm entrepreneurs, Danes consistently advocate a more sustainable EU in the policy-making process. Since the 1970s, the EU has taken up environmental matters—even though these were not specified in the Treaty of Rome. The European Court of Justice has played an active role in agenda setting, and several important decisions have involved Danish rights to maintain particular practices. Denmark's leadership in the EU presidency (2002) engaged specific national concerns—from environmental issues to strengthening human rights and democracy as part of the enlargement criteria of the EU. As Europe determines how the environment should be governed, sustainability is also on the agenda of Scandinavians outside the EU.

ECO-POLITICS IN NORWAY AND ICELAND: SUSTAINABILITY IN PRACTICE

The two western Scandinavian states, Norway and Iceland, are dependent on the resources of the sea for their prosperity. Each of these societies has engaged in seafaring, fishing, and whaling for centuries. Yet as other countries industrialized and became less dependent on the resources of the sea, attitudes about acceptable and unacceptable practices fundamentally changed. According to public opinion studies, approximately 75 percent of the adult population in Norway and Iceland support a pro-whaling policy, whereas in other societies (particularly the United States and Europe) whaling is considered an undesirable activity.[23] However, as a matter of principle and a defense of economic interests and identity, the Norwegian and Icelandic governments permit "sustainable whaling" to continue—even though international society views whaling as reprehensible. Norm entrepreneurship, in this case, requires these governments to resist the "emotional," "unscientific" criticisms made by societies that are "out of touch with nature."[24]

When national governments met in Washington, D.C., to create the first international regime to regulate the environment (the International Whaling Convention [IWC]) in 1946, Norway and Iceland were among the founding members. However, as the regime has evolved, these governments criticize the way its mission has changed. According to IWC rules, a three-fourths majority is required for all commission decisions. Since the 1972 Stockholm Conference on the Environment, the whale has become the symbol of the necessity to protect the environment. Environmental groups launched a major campaign to curtail whaling and encouraged states to join the IWC and protest the practice of whale hunting. When more and more anti-whaling states joined the IWC, the balance within the organization shifted against whaling. The IWC no longer exists to protect the interests of the whaling industry and enable limited, sustainable catches but has instead adopted a much more restrictive stance prohibiting whaling except under very limited circumstances.[25]

In 1982, when the IWC adopted a moratorium on commercial whaling (to be put into effect in 1985), the Norwegians made a formal objection. The

Norwegians agreed to investigate the size of whaling stocks before resuming the whale hunt. In 1988, Norway, Iceland, the Faroe Islands, and Greenland formed a regional whale management group outside the IWC called the North Atlantic Marine Mammal Commission. And in 1993, the Norwegian government made an independent decision to resume whaling in accordance with Article V of the International Convention for the Regulation of Whaling. Members of the international community and environmental organizations denounced Norway as a violator of international agreements. However, in the Norwegian view, the intent of the convention is "not to protect the whales for their own sake, but to regulate catches of whales for the benefit of mankind both now and in the future."[26] Principled arguments are made in defense of whaling—even though only a few hundred minke whales are hunted each year by a group of fishermen who supplement their annual income by diversifying their catch. The Norwegians distinguish between harvesting minke whales (which they argue are abundant and not in danger of extinction), as opposed to blue or bowhead whales, which are underpopulated and endangered. For Norwegians and Icelanders, the IWC has lost its institutional legitimacy by allowing environmentalists to dictate the rules governing whaling. When Keiko the Orca whale was returned by airplane to Icelandic waters, the norms of how others view marine mammals appeared absurd to a nation of fishermen who still enjoy an occasional whale steak.

Accession to the EU appears elusive for both the Norwegians and Icelanders for the foreseeable future. However, as members of the Nordic Council, the ministers of the environment (Sweden, Denmark, Norway, Iceland, and Finland) meet three times a year and have a back channel to the EU by articulating common interests multilaterally. In addition, these governments actively work for tighter environmental standards and more sustainable practices as members of the UN, where they can partner with others (including the EU) to exert pressure on states with more neoliberal views of how industry should be governed, such as the United States, Canada, and Australia.[27]

Thus, Scandinavia has not been silenced in the process of integrating with its largest trading partner. Finland and Sweden traded off neutrality for engagement yet have specified in the EU's security structures how security arrangements should respond to new types of threats (the Petersberg Tasks outlined in the Amsterdam Treaty). Denmark's resistance is a constant reminder that the EU is a centralized system, where the voice of the people may be lost. Responding to the "democratic deficit" has become a part of the EU's agenda—because of the role of the Danes and as a part of the Swedish EU presidency. Norway and Iceland will be the last Scandinavians to join the EU's regional governance structure and are not willing to be passive actors in determining how sustainability functions in practice. Any efforts to bring the

Icelanders and Norwegians on board will have to engage different systems of management for marine resources than the EU has adopted to date.

We have seen how Scandinavia influences the most powerful regional actor in world politics. By being at the table in the EU's institutional structure, they have the capacity to influence others and to set the agenda. However, as the next chapter demonstrates, the Swedes, Finns, and Danes are restrained in their foreign-policy making because they are legally bound to maintain the EU's position, whereas the Norwegians maintain a unique degree of freedom, permitting some innovative developments in their country's international relations.

NOTES

1. See Andrew Moravscik, *The Choice for Europe: Social Purpose and State Power from Messina to Maastricht* (Ithaca, NY: Cornell University Press, 1998).

2. Laurent Goetschel, "The Foreign and Security Interests of Small States in Today's Europe," in *Small States Inside and Outside the European Union: Interests and Policies* (Boston: Kluwar Academy Publishers, 1998), p. 19, cited in Jessie Keough, "Visions of Europe: Small States and European Policies: The Influence of Finland and Sweden upon the European Union's Agenda," paper presented at the University of Washington, June 12, 2001, p. 3.

3. Conference proceedings, "Scandinavia in Europe," University of Washington, Seattle, February 2001, and discussions with Johan Lilliehook, visiting EU expert from Sweden.

4. Austria, Switzerland, and Portugal also joined EFTA in 1959.

5. See James Caporaso, "Across the Great Divide: Integrating Comparative and International Politics," *International Studies Quarterly* 41 (1997): 584.

6. See Lene Hansen and Ole Wæver (eds.), *European Integration and National Identity: The Challenge of the Nordic States* (London: Routledge, 2002), and Christine Ingebritsen, *The Nordic States and European Unity* (Ithaca, NY: Cornell University Press, 1998) for an understanding of Nordic patterns of accession to the EU.

7. William Taylor and Paul Cole, *Nordic Defense: Comparative Decision Making* (Lexington, KY: DC Heath and Company, 1985), p. 38.

8. Swedish representative to the WTO meeting held in Seattle, Washington.

9. David Arter, "Small State Influence within the EU: The Case of Finland's 'Northern Dimension Initiative,'" *Journal of Common Market Studies* 38 (2000): 685.

10. Arter, "Small State Influence within the EU," p. 693.

11. See "A Northern Dimension for the Policies of the Union," communication from the Commission (EU: November 1998) and "The Implementation of a Northern Dimension for the Policies of the European Union," conclusions adopted by the European Council of Ministers on May 31, 1999.

12. Ariane Sains, "Sweden Takes the EU Helm," *Europe*, no. 402 (December/January 2000–2001): 6.

13. Annica Kronsell, "Can Small States Influence EU Norms? Insights from Sweden's Participation in the Field of Environmental Politics," working paper presented at the Conference "The EU and Scandinavia Today," The EU Center of Seattle, University of Washington, Seattle, February 1–2, 2001, p. 5.

14. Annica Kronsell, "Can Small States Influence EU Norms?" p. 10.

15. Presentation by Anita Gradin, Swedish representative to the EU, Spring 2001, University of Washington, Seattle.

16. Royal Danish Ministry of Foreign Affairs, "One Europe: Programme of the Danish Presidency of the EU, Second Half of 2002" (Copenhagen, 2002), p. 8.

17. Sains, "Sweden Takes the EU Helm," p. 6.

18. *The Economist*, "Jens Stoltenberg: Cautious PM," July 22, 2000.

19. Eldborg Lower, "Defence Policy Challenges for the Year 2000," Oslo: Norwegian Ministry of Defense, http://odin.dep.no, 1/18/2001, p. 4.

20. See Magne Barthe and Else Marie Brodshaug, *Nordisk sikkerhet—paa vei mot EU og NATO* (Oslo: Institut for Fedsforskning, 1997), pp. 19–21.

21. Henrik Bering, "Denmark, the Euro, and the Fear of the Foreign," *Policy Review*, no. 104 (December 2000): 1.

22. Discussions with James Caporaso, EU expert, March 12, 2002, Seattle, Washington.

23. Gisli Palsson and E. Paul Durrenberger, *Images of Contemporary Iceland* (Iowa City: University of Iowa Press, 1996), p. 26.

24. Interviews conducted in Norway and Iceland, Spring 2000.

25. See Herluf Sigvaldsson, "The International Whaling Commission: The Transition from a 'Whaling Club' to a 'Preservationist Club,'" *Cooperation and Conflict* 31, no. 3 (1996): 320.

26. Norwegian Ministry of Foreign Affairs, "Norwegian Minke Whaling," Oslo, 1995, p. 4.

27. Torkil Sorensen, "Rent Miljo—en nordisk maerkesag," *Politik I Norden* no. 2 (March/April 2001): 11–12.

· 4 ·

Norway's Niche in World Politics

$\mathcal{N}$orway, situated north of Denmark and west of the largest of the Scandinavian states (Sweden), has built an international reputation that defies its small population size, economic might, and military capacity. Even though Sweden is described as the "most internationalist Scandinavian state,"[1] Norway has cultivated a unique niche in world politics—unburdened by many contradictions confronting its larger neighbor to the east. With the end of the Cold War, Swedes suffered a collective identity crisis. No longer considered the leading model of welfare capitalism (with growing unemployment and budget deficits), Swedes confronted the limits of neutrality, revealed by the government's secret plan to cooperate with NATO in case of war, and encountered the challenges of pooled sovereignty in the EU.[2] Much to the dismay of prominent Swedes, many of the Scandinavian innovations in international politics are credited to Norwegian diplomacy and individual leaders who have made a difference in world politics. And each year, when the Nobel Peace Prize is awarded, international attention focuses on Oslo.

How and why has Norway developed this role, and what are the implications of embedding the state and society in different forms of international cooperation for structuring the agenda in world politics? This chapter examines these questions and offers several examples of innovative Norwegian leadership—from human rights to international peacekeeping.

WHAT MAKES NORWAY
EXCEPTIONAL NEXT TO ITS NEIGHBORS?

Petroleum analysts refer to the Norwegians as "the blue-eyed Arabs of the north." The affluence of Norway in recent decades has given the state and society new options in a world where secure supplies of oil and gas are increasingly precious, and global demand is far from waning. Norway is responsible for 2 percent of the world's oil production, and petroleum is the state's largest net export. Enriching the people of Norway with prosperity and creating new possibilities of wealth enables the government and society to support a global presence that would otherwise be untenable.

While natural resources provide the structural conditions for Norway's capacity to play a global role, the foreign policy priorities of the state in international politics express enduring values of the society and government that preceded the riches of the oil era. Even before the discovery of oil and gas, Norwegians were known internationally for innovative diplomatic solutions to international crises.

Norwegian foreign policy has a missionary quality, strengthened by a strong sense of nationalism that coincided with becoming independent after hundreds of years of subordination to two more powerful neighbors (Denmark, 1450–1814; Sweden, 1814–1905). Most importantly, however, exceptional individuals embodying (and, in some cases, defining) the core values of Norwegian society have brought international recognition to this rugged territory that extends north of the Arctic Circle and shares borders with Sweden (1,619 km), Finland (721 km), and Russia (196 km). Most of the "norm entrepreneurship" can be traced to those individuals representing the Social Democratic Party, the most important party in Norwegian political history (see table 4.1). Norwegian social democracy had a more radical agenda than Swedish social democracy. Nor were Social Democrats as liberal-minded in Norway as they were in Denmark.[3] Since the ascendance of Prime Minister Kjell Magne Bondevik, the Christian People's Party has assumed a prominent position in promoting its vision of international activism, which is based on religious values and emphasizes the importance of home, family, church, poor assistance, and human rights.

The following discussion examines how and why Norway has cultivated a niche in world politics—from its independence in 1905 to the present. Neighboring Sweden, with almost twice the population and an equally persistence agenda in its foreign relations, has been unable to achieve the successes in international diplomacy associated with Norwegian interventions.

Table 4.1. Norwegian Social Democrats: Prominent Leaders

DNA=Norwegian Labor Party; H=Conservative Party; Sp=Center Party; KrF=Christian People's Party; FrP=Progress Party; SV=Socialist Left Party

Prime Ministers	Tenure in Office	Party
Einar Gerhardsen	June 29, 1945–Nov 15, 1951	DNA
Oscar Torp	Nov 15, 1951–Jan 20, 1955	DNA
Einar Gerhardsen	Jan 21, 1955–Aug 27, 1963	DNA
John Lyng	Aug 27, 1963–Sept 25, 1963	
Einar Gerhardsen	Sept 25, 1963–Oct 12, 1965	DNA
Per Borten	Oct 12–March 13, 1971	Sp
Trygve Bratteli	Mar 13, 1971–Oct 7, 1972	DNA
Lars Korvald	Oct 7, 1972–Oct 14, 1973	KrF
Trygve Bratteli	Oct 14, 1973–Jan 12, 1976	DNA
Odvar Nordli	Jan 12, 1976–Feb 4, 1981	DNA
Gro Harlem Brundtland	Feb 4, 1981–Oct 14, 1981	DNA
Kare Willoch	Oct 14, 1981–May 9, 1986	H
Gro Harlem Brundtland	May 9, 1986–Oct 16, 1989	DNA
Jan Syse	Oct 16, 1989–Nov 3, 1990	H
Gro Harlem Brundtland	Nov 3, 1990–Oct 25, 1996	DNA
Thorbjorn Jagland	Oct 25, 1996–Oct 17, 1997	DNA
Kjell Magne Bondevik	Oct 17, 1997–Mar 17, 2000	KrF
Jens Stoltenberg	Mar 17, 2000–Oct 19, 2001	DNA
Kjell Magne Bondevik	Oct 19, 2001–?	KrF

Source: www.terra.es/personal2/monolith/Norway.htm.

THE NANSEN PASSPORT

Fridtjof Nansen (1861–1930) was a polar explorer, zoologist, artist, and statesman. He earned an international reputation for his Arctic expeditions, and became a global figure in the early twentieth century as a consequence of his persistent and innovative humanitarian relief work. According to historian Oystein Sorensen, Fridtjof Nansen is Norway's most famous international figure, and Nansen himelf worked to cultivate his own image. Through visual media (his own drawings, photographic representations, and paintings), Nansen himself perpetuated the myth of the national hero.[4] As Roland Huntford argues,

> Nansen's own High Norse appearance was unashamedly exploited. Around the turn of the century there was a state-subsidised, popular illustrated edition of the Norse sagas. One of the illustrators was Nansen's particular

friend among the Lysaker Circle, an accomplished draughtsman called Erik Werenskiold. He very recognizably used Nansen as a model for some of the medieval Norwegian heroes. That neatly symbolized Nansen's elevation to a national totem.[5]

Nansen's life history paralleled the rise of modern Norway. He was born to distinguished parents and showed an early interest in scientific discovery. At age twenty-two he went on an expedition to the east coast of Greenland. He documented his voyage in drawings and writings. Motivated by scientific curiosity and a desire to continue his adventures on sea and ice, Nansen led a party of six on skis across Greenland in 1888. Surviving difficult conditions for two months, the trip attracted international attention. However, Nansen's three-year expedition on the *Fram* (a polar vessel that was specifically built for Nansen to withstand the pressure of Arctic ice) won the hearts of the Norwegian people. When he returned, he received a hero's welcome in Christiana (now Oslo). His fame spread to Britain, where he was asked to present his findings at prominent social clubs and scholarly meetings.

Because of his international connections and widespread support at home, Nansen became an important figure, supporting Norway's independence from Sweden. "Using his diplomatic skills and his prestige, he helped obtain world recognition of Norway as an independent state."[6] When Norwegians initiated an internal debate concerning the appropriateness of retaining the Swedish–Norwegian union, Nansen played a mediating role. A coalition of prominent leaders (including Christian Michelsen of Bergen) began advocating independence. Nansen joined Michelsen in the call for independence and rejected the idea of a republic in favor of a monarchy. Relying on his reputation abroad, he made the case for Norwegian independence overseas—particularly in Britain, where he enjoyed widespread support.

When Norway broke away peacefully from Sweden in 1905, Nansen played a leading role. In his words, "any union in which one people is restrained in exercising its freedom is and will remain a danger."[7] Nansen was sent to Denmark to request that Prince Charles accept the position of king of Norway under the name Haakon. Prince Charles was married to England's Princess Maud, an important foreign policy connection for an emerging small state. Prince Charles agreed to serve, as long as a majority of the Norwegian people favored his ascendance to the throne.

Nansen became Norway's diplomatic representative to London (1906–1908), and in 1920 was asked to serve as the Norwegian representative to the League of Nations. It was within the league that Nansen pioneered innovative solutions to pressing transnational problems. As Russians faced a severe crisis, Nansen created an international relief office in Moscow. He first appealed to the league for assistance, and when it was not forthcoming,

Nansen raised the necessary funds from private sources.[8] In 1922, under Nansen's leadership, an international agreement was adopted in Geneva to create "Nansen passports" for displaced persons. Approximately 500,000 refugees were returned to their homeland relying on Nansen's humanitarian solution.

Because of his leadership, Nansen received the Nobel Peace Prize in 1922, and the Nansen International Office for Refugees received the Peace Prize in 1938. At the award ceremony, Fredrik Stang, chairman of the Nobel Committee, made the following remarks honoring Nansen's service:

> We have seen how great international tasks have again and again been entrusted to Nansen. We have seen him appear as the High Commissioner of the League of Nations, its representative and plenipotentiary. We have seen him negotiating with representatives of nearly every country in Europe or with agencies created under his administration. We have seen him incessantly on the move: one day we read in a cable that he is having talks with Lloyd George in London; then we suddenly learn that he has gone to Rome for a conference with the Pope.[9]

Nansen's leadership enabled the repatriation of tens of thousands of prisoners displaced by war between Russia and Germany. He also played a critical role in providing famine relief by negotiating the delivery of grain to Russia and urging the League of Nations to provide credit to the Russian state to prevent people from dying of starvation. His opponents voiced political concerns about whether the aid would get to those who needed it; yet Nansen persisted, based on principles of human rights and compassion for the people of Russia. He convinced the Norwegian government, other European states, and private donors to provide aid to avert the crisis.

Nansen also played a critical role in the aftermath of the Greek–Turkish War. Displaced persons from that conflict were also repatriated, relying on Nansen's leadership. In reflecting on Nansen's contributions, Fredrik Stang noted:

> Perhaps what has most impressed all of us is his ability to stake his life time and time again on a single idea, on one thought, and to inspire others to follow him. We remember a young boy, for he was but little more than that, crossing Greenland on skis. He thought that up . . . in the North where the costly expeditions from great nations always suffered shipwreck, Norwegian sports equipment and Norwegian familiarity with ice and snow would be able to succeed. He did succeed, and his trip became a landmark in the history of Arctic exploration. We recall too a mature man, who on the basis of his scientific knowledge, developed the theory that a current flows from east to west across the Polar Sea. Nearly all the scientists

believed that he was wrong. But he staked his life on the theory; he allowed himself to be frozen into the eastern ice to be carried over the Pole. The current was there and carried him forward to his goal. And is it not much the same thing that we have now witnessed? An undercurrent in which few have believed has again carried Nansen forward: the deep current of human feeling which lies beneath the layer of ice in which nations and individuals encase themselves during the daily struggles and the trials of life. He believed in this current and because he did, his work has triumphed. May this current also carry much for the future![10]

The legacy of Nansen's work is still visible in contemporary international relations. As explained by Thorvald Stoltenberg, "In the refugee area, the rudiments of international protection, first conceived by Nansen, have developed into an elaborate legal framework."[11] Principles of human rights are codified in UN resolutions and efforts to repatriate migrants and refugees remain central tasks for international agencies, including the UN High Commissioner for Refugees. The Nansen School, located in Lillehammer, Norway, is a humanist institution that maintains centers of conflict resolution in five areas of former Yugoslavia, thereby keeping Nansen's legacy alive. As Sidney Tarrow argues, Nansen represents a rooted cosmopolitan, or transnational activist, who carries values embedded in the nation-state to the world community.

Nansen's legacy has also inspired other Norwegians to challenge the boundaries of existing forms of international cooperation. As one observer noted in praise of Knut Vollebaek's ascendance to the chairmanship of the Organization for Security Cooperation in Europe (OSCE), "Norwegian diplomacy is known for its creativity, dynamism and ability to globally assess European and world security. I wish it every success for our common good."[12] Political choices (NATO membership, opting for the European Free Trade Area and the European Economic Area [EEA] over EU membership) differ from neighboring states and have both constrained and enabled Norwegian political authorities. Participation in international institutions has given Norway a voice, yet it has not compromised national sovereignty to the same degree as has occurred in Finland and Sweden. Nonetheless, when the EU makes a decision, Norway is required to respond—like it or not.

Membership in the EU requires governments to participate in common policies at the region level—from agricultural policy to tariff arrangements, and security policy. By resisting membership in the EU (once in 1972 and again in 1994), Norway has sought to cooperate closely with the EU about foreign policy yet lacks the presence in decision-making forums available to the Danes, Swedes, and Finns. However, Norway's aloofness from formal participation in the EU has certain advantages, and the Norwegians have cultivated a niche as *global* actors, while still pursuing particular new forms of regional cooperation.

NORWAY'S GLOBAL ROLE IN PURSUING PEACE

One example of Norway's unique role in international relations is innovation in international peacekeeping and conflict resolution. The international reputation Norwegians have earned in bringing the leaders of Israel and the Palestine Liberation Organization (PLO) to the negotiating table and concluding the Oslo Accord has generated goodwill and political capital—even though the region has suffered major setbacks in achieving peace. Norway's intervention represented decades of cultivating close ties in the region, the participation of nongovernmental organizations (NGOs), and entrepreneurial leadership of a group of prominent Norwegians (Terje Rød-Larsen, Marianne Heiberg, and Johan Jorgen Holst). With the end of the Cold War, Norway's participation in global peacekeeping activities (from Guatemala to Colombia) rely on the model developed in the Middle East: depend on neutral parties to inform officials about an opening, initiate closer cooperation between the opposing parties (preferably in secret), establish trust, and agree to a set of basic principles, relying on Norwegians as mediators.

Norway's role in conflict resolution is not new. The policy is consistent with a "bridge-building" strategy, defined as playing the role of mediator between opposing powers in international relations.[13] Norway, whenever possible, has sought to dissipate conflict and promote peace. The failure of the League of Nations in averting war and Germany's occupation of Norway during World War II were collective experiences that contributed to the belief that neutrality was not a viable option. Yet, it was prominent foreign-policy makers who ushered in a new era of Norwegian activism. Trygve Lie, who replaced Halvdan Koht as foreign minister in the Labor Government (in exile) in 1941, helped define and implement a new, internationalist orientation in Norwegian foreign policy. As Philip Burgess has argued, Trygve Lie expressed the view that security in the period following World War II was conditional on international cooperation and participation of the great powers in international organizations.[14] Lie outlined a role for Norway in the postwar period relying on the concept of *brobyggning* or bridge building: "The smaller nations have a great part to play in cementing the peace. They are disinterested in many political disputes; their ambitions are cultural and economic . . . their foreign policy should aim at making a sincere contribution to the mutual understanding and confidence of the great powers."[15] As Trygve Lie stated in a speech to the Norwegian Parliament on June 19, 1945, "Norway must seek to obtain security in an organized cooperation with other peoples."[16]

Norway's multilateral strategy relied on cooperation with other Nordic governments, participation in the UN, and a restricted partnership with NATO. Norway's foreign policy sought to dissipate conflict between the great powers, and in particular to avoid isolating the Soviet Union. The ideas that Trygve Lie expressed in the Norwegian Parliament and his experience as a diplomat of a small European state became important in his new role as the first secretary-general of the UN.

Precisely because of his Norwegian identity and experience, Lie was the appropriate candidate at a critical moment in international institution building. Lie was trained as a lawyer, served as foreign minister, and was a member of the Norwegian Social Democratic Party. In contrast to other candidates, Lie was acceptable to members of the Western bloc and to leaders of the Soviet Union. With Trygve Lie's accession as UN secretary-general, it could be credibly argued that no one power could dominate the organization.[17] Lie headed the UN during a tense period in global politics (1946–1953), and he played an important role as a broker between the West and the Soviet Union. He brought to the position an understanding of small-state political experience and the necessity to bind more powerful states into international cooperation as a means of mitigating conflict.[18] He paved the way for another Scandinavian, Dag Hammarskjold, by his willingness to interpret broadly the mission of the general-secretary and to engage in private consultations and negotiations in the pursuit of peace.

During the East-West conflict, Norway advocated empathy with the Soviet Union, yet allied itself militarily with the United States as a member of NATO and through special, bilateral military agreements. The combination of "reassurance" and "deterrence" strategies is found throughout the Nordic area, yet Norway capitalized on this experience by exporting this foreign policy tradition to other areas of the globe.

Although efforts to negotiate a settlement between Israel and the Palestinians were underway in Washington, D.C., the Norwegians established another informal means of bringing the parties together that eventually led to the Oslo Accord, a declaration of principles signed by Yitzhak Rabin and Yasser Arafat on September 13, 1993. The process was initiated by members of the Norwegian Institute of Applied Social Sciences (FAFO), but the Norwegian government made it possible for the parties to meet in secret.[19] A group of Norwegian researchers investigating the living conditions in the West Bank and the Gaza Strip interacted with Israelis and Palestinians and found that there was interest on both sides for cooperation. The level of violence in the Gaza Strip had escalated, the PLO and its leadership were under criticism, and the Labor Party in Israel had made a campaign promise to take steps to resolve the conflict.[20]

Norwegian foreign minister Johan Jørgen Holst cooperated with social scientist Terje Rød Larsen, director of FAFO, to create a secret channel of negotiations initiated in January 1993. The important players were advisors to Arafat and Rabin, who were able to meet informally and develop personal ties that facilitated trust and mutual understanding. These included Israeli academics Yair Hirschfield and Ron Pundak, PLO treasurer Abu Ala, and Uri Savir, the director-general of the Israeli Foreign Ministry. Precisely because the negotiations occurred in private, among a small group of participants, without the pressures of domestic politics or the presence of the media, conditions were more favorable to taking risks and making concessions. From a preliminary discussion between the parties of economic motivations for cooperation, the parties eventually agreed to a set of common principles, expressed in the Oslo Accord.

The Oslo Accord begins with a statement of mutual recognition between Israel and the PLO. The basis for the mutual recognition was written in the form of letters exchanged between Rabin and Arafat. In Rabin's letter, he stated that the government of Israel had decided to recognize the PLO as the representative of the Palestinian people and to begin negotiations with the PLO.[21] By recognizing the PLO as a legitimate partner in the peace process, Rabin took a major, historic step—one that ultimately cost him his life.

The Oslo Accord also includes a Declaration of Principles, with an agenda for negotiating Palestinian self-rule in the occupied territories. Following the initial accord, another more detailed document of approximately three hundred pages was agreed on, delineating Israeli and Palestinian zones in the West Bank.

In recent years, the outbreaks of violence in the region have intensified. Many observers fear that the successes achieved by Norwegian negotiators have been lost. However, the Oslo Accord has a legacy that persists, even though the conflict endures. All efforts to pursue peace have a reference point: Oslo permitted the parties to move forward in an atmosphere of trust and mutual respect. It is internationally recognized as a historic breakthrough in the relationship between opposing parties and is a reminder of what is possible in international politics.

Most notably, the Oslo Accord could not have been achieved without the intervention of a small state such as Norway. As Jan Egeland has argued in *Impotent Superpower—Potent Small State* (1988), the United States is burdened with its role in world politics and divided internally. U.S. foreign policy is full of contradictions and lacks the coherence of the institutionally centralized Norwegian state. In Norway, a small group of foreign policy makers ngstanding tradition of seeking consensus have been better able to resp~ to external events in a cohesive and decisive manner.[22] The differences between the United States and Norway are not only defined by relative power and the degree of centralized institutions, but are also ideological. Active participation in conflict mediation (even in areas far from Norway) has evolved from the country's experience in international relations and the ideas of prominent foreign policy makers (such as Fridtjof Nansen, Halvdan Koht, Trygve Lie, Thorvald Stoltenberg, Johan Jørgen Holst, Gro Harlem Brundtland, and Knut Vollebaek).

The United States, in contrast to Norway, has been willing but unable to bring the parties to a negotiated settlement. The United States is frequently accused of meddling, pursuing its own strategic interests, or obeying powerful lobbying groups in American society in its Middle East policy. However, asking the United States to stand aside is absurd. As one observer put it, "It is the same as asking the sun to keep out of the earth's business."[23] This analysis and Jan Egeland's study suggest that small states are better situated than more powerful states to forge these kinds of deals in international relations in the quiet corner of northern Europe.

As Thorvald Stoltenberg argues, the Oslo breakthrough was cultivated over many decades of engagement in the region.[24] In a speech made at his alma mater, the Columbia University School of International and Public Affairs on September 28, 1993, Johan Jorgen Holst outlined five reasons why Norway was accepted as a legitimate partner in the Middle East Peace Process: (1) The historic ties between the Israeli and Norwegian Labor Parties encouraged trust and inspired confidence; (2) Norway had a well-established reputation as being evenhanded and professional because of participation in numerous UN peacekeeping initiatives; (3) Norwegians had developed an extensive network of contacts among the PLO and Israelis; (4) Norway had a small inner circle of dedicated and qualified experts; and (5) precisely because Norway was an unexpected partner, it was possible to maintain secrecy.[25] According to Holst, the setting of the talks also contributed to informal interaction: smaller locations were selected, with opportunities for negotiators to spend their spare time together. All meetings were conducted in English, which eliminated the time and interpretative ambiguities created by reliance on translators. In an account of cultural differences between the parties, Holst explained how the negotiations would become stalemated periodically. As the parties attempted to show resolve, engage in brinkmanship and theater, the Middle East style of bargaining contrasted sharply with the style of "level-headed and even-tempered Norwegians raised in a tradition of consensus oriented bargaining."[26]

Although numerous conditions were necessary to permit the parties to agree to the terms of the Oslo Accord, it would not have been possible to achieve this international agreement without the engagement and commitment of prominent foreign policy makers and the dedication of a team of Norwegians: Johan Jørgen Holst, Dr. Marianne Heiberg, State Secretary Jan Egeland, Terje-Rød Larsen (director, FAFO) and Mona Jul (Ministry of Foreign Affairs).

To what extent does Norway's participation in Middle East peace negotiations serve as a model for intervention in other conflicts? Norway has earned a reputation in international peacekeeping, and, according to representatives from the Ministry of Foreign Affairs, there have been more and more requests for Norwegian diplomats to serve as a third party in negotiations. In selective cases, Norway has been willing to intervene—under three conditions: the involvement must be consistent with previous peace initiatives; local experts (preferably an NGO) must be available; and there must be access to prominent contacts on each side of the conflict.[27] In Sri Lanka, Sudan, the former Yugoslavia, Colombia, and Guatemala, Norwegians have become involved in international peacekeeping activities. When the Tamil rebels in Sri Lanka consistently challenged the authority of the government, it was a team of Norwegian diplomats who coordinated the first peace negotiations held in seven years during the spring of 2002.[28] As Norwegian foreign policy expert Jan Egeland says, humanitarian assistance may lead to Norwegian involvement in a particular area of the world and eventually provide the conditions appropriate for extending Norway's involvement in the form of peacekeeping activities.

This chapter identifies enduring patterns of Norwegian participation in international politics, specific Norwegians who have made a difference in foreign-policy making and have forged a peacekeeping identity for Norway. Norway has made initiatives in international relations that defy its status as a militarily weak, economically dependent small state in world politics. In promoting its values outside its borders and establishing new forums for international peacekeeping, the Norwegians exercise "social power" in international relations.

Jan Egeland summarizes Norway's role in international politics in the following way: "Our hope and aim is that small countries can be honest brokers in the international arena, often cooperating with the bigger powers, and always available to parties in conflict. We have a small stick and a small carrot, but we very often have the trust of the parties."[29]

Although the prospects for peace in the Middle East have deteriorated, the Oslo Accord set an important precedent. The Norwegians successfully brought the parties to the table; facilitated informal contacts between Israeli and PLO representatives; provided a framework for resolution; and encouraged open and direct exchange between the opposing parties. The Oslo Accord codified a mutual agreement on fundamental rights. It did not resolve the deeply held divisions over Gaza or Jericho, nor can it overcome the domestic stalemate in Israeli politics. However, the Oslo Accord remains the benchmark. It provides an institutional memory of what is possible—and parameters for further cooperation.

The price of peace is not inconsequential, particularly for smaller actors in international politics. Yet Norwegians are willing to pay, as demonstrated by the government's pledge in October 1993, to provide $35 million dollars to the Middle East peace process over a five-year period.[30]

In contrast to the predictions of political realists (states pursue self-interest in an anarchic international system), Norway seeks international conflict resolution in an area of the world where it would be in its material interest to remain disengaged.

Under the leadership of Gro Harlem Brundtland, the global agenda has been structured in two issues-areas, the environment and health policy.

BRUNDTLAND: FROM OUR COMMON FUTURE TO THE WORLD HEALTH ORGANIZATION

Gro Harlem Brundtland was born in Oslo in 1939 and entered national politics at the age of thirty. Brundtland became a prominent member of the Norwegian Social Democratic Party and Norway's minister of the environment (1974–1979). Brundtland attracted international attention as Norway's first female prime minister (1981, 1986–1989) and by appointing women to 50 percent of the cabinet. She married Arne Olav Brundtland, leader of the Conservative Party, and eventually convinced him to change his political affiliation. Brundtland originally studied medicine at the University of Oslo and continued her studies at Harvard University.[31] When she resigned from office in the 1990s, she expressed concern that young men in Norway might be growing up with the idea that only women can lead the government.

In international relations, Brundtland also charted new territory. As the leader of the UN Commission on the Environment, her team produced the report *Our Common Future*. The report codified an enduring norm of environmental cooperation, "sustainable development." Under Brundtland's leadership, the Norwegians engaged in a fierce national debate over the pros and cons of entering the EU (1991–1994). In a close vote, a majority of Norwegians (52.5 percent) rejected Prime Minister Brundtland's call to join the EU. Yet, during her tenure in office, the diplomatic community worked tirelessly to bring Norway as close as possible to the institutions and policies of EU member-states. In fact, the Norwegian media criticized the government for creating a "virtual" EU state.

In 1992, Norway became an associate member of the Western European Union. Brundtland's legacy of "Europe through the back door" was sustained by Minister of Foreign Affairs Thorbjorn Jagland, who advocated Norwegian accession (even after the national vote), and announced to the Norwegian Parliament his support for fully engaging in new forms of regional cooperation—including assistance in the creation of a common European security and defense policy.[32] And even though Norway is not a EU member, it is a part of the Schengen Agreement to collectively manage the EU's borders. Brundltland's legacy continues, as she brings new agendas to WHO and restructures the provision of global health policy.

Since Brundtland's resignation from national politics, Norway has increasingly come under scrutiny for attitudes found elsewhere in Europe—from the Netherlands to Denmark to France—favoring the "national" over the "multicultural" vision of society. Norway is struggling to balance an activist international agenda and a resistance to globalism within Norwegian society.

CONTRADICTIONS AT HOME:
NORWEGIANS RESIST INTERNATIONALISM

As the Norwegian state and society engage a more integrated Europe, and a global international economy introduces new ways of living, working, and conducting business, Norwegians have engaged in a period of self-reflection. The most contentious issue Norway faces is the emergence of a multi-ethnic society. As Thomas Hylland Eriksen states,

> although the country has admitted relatively few immigrants and refugees in comparison to, for example, Sweden or France, the new ethnic minorities are putting their marks on the bigger towns and cities. Five per cent of the Norwegian population was born abroad, half of them outside Europe. Will they always be an exotic foreign element or is it possible to create a Norwegian identity with for instance, ample room for Asian Moslems?[33]

Confronted with more international influences culturally, economically, and in its political relations with the EU, Norwegians are having difficulty overcoming the tendency of the society to marginalize those who do not conform to accepted ways of interacting. Domestic strife over immigrants is highly visible in the print and visual media and in preferences for political parties. For example, on national holidays and at many wedding celebrations, participants wear regional costumes, hand sewn and ornately decorated. The editor of the Norwegian handicrafts magazine, Nina Granlund Saether, told an audience in an interview that non-Norwegians should not be allowed to wear or make the *bunad*, Norway's traditional costume.[34] The head of Norway's parliamentary committee promoting a multicultural society, Anne Kari Lande Hasle, rejected her position as out of step with twenty-first–century politics. The growing support for Norway's right wing anti-immigration party (the Progress Party) also shows a lack of tolerance for "the other" in national politics.

As a consistent advocate for human rights abroad, Norwegian government officials have pursued a variety of measures to counter intolerance at home. Norway has taken steps to adopt principles outlined in the International Convention on the Elimination of All Forms of Racial Discrimination in Norwegian law and has created a separate measure to prohibit ethnic discrimination.[35] The government sees its efforts as both domestic and international: "If Norway criticizes violations of human rights abroad, Norway also must be willing to discuss any problems the country may have in observing these rights within its borders."[36] Included on Norway's agenda for human rights are integrating human rights and development policy; ensuring the rights of the child; banning reliance on capital punishment; promoting the rights of women; protecting the rights of single-sex couples; eliminating discrimination based on race, ethnicity, or religion; and prohibiting torture.

As further examples of state activism to combat violence at home, Prime Minister Kjell Magne Bondevik introduced a new set of anti-bullying measures in Norwegian society in 2002. "Bullying" refers to repeated acts of verbal, physical, or other forms of torment designed to inflict injury or harm on others.[37] Norwegians were shocked by incidences of suicide by teenage boys tormented by their peers. By formally acknowledging violence in schools and the tormenting of children by others, Norwegians were the first in the world to develop social policy measures to prevent bullying in schools.

In foreign-policy making, the Bondevik government has, again, demonstrated the unique position of Norway in international relations. When U.S.-European relations deteriorated in the spring of 2003, in response to an American-led military intervention in Iraq, the Norwegian government volunteered to mediate between the EU and the United States. President Bush accepted the prime minister's invitation to visit Oslo in May 2003. In addition, Norwegians seek to play a role in helping rebuild Iraq in the aftermath of the war—a step that the government can make independently, outside the official channels of the EU and consistent with a longstanding policy of supporting peace and human rights and providing generous forms of development assistance.

Norway, in contrast with its neighbors, has received much international attention for peacekeeping and norm entrepreneurship. For example, a prominent article in the *New York Times* (2002) described Norway as the "international capital of peace." Norwegian diplomats are trusted partners in conflict resolution because "it does not carry its olive branch across reservoirs of bad blood . . . rather, the Norwegian government and Norwegian charities have financed so much humanitarian work in volatile countries that Norway is often a welcome guest in those places."[38] The Norwegian government continuously receives honors and recognition for its global role in conflict resolution efforts around the world—from Sudan to Sri Lanka.

However, there are contradictions to this global role as Norwegian society becomes more international. In recent decades, the rise of electoral support for the Progressive Party (with a more restrictive immigration policy) is evidence of a shift away from social democratic internationalism. Xenophobia and discrimination are difficult to legislate against, yet may have profound domestic and international consequences for Norwegian society and politics. The anti-globalists in Norwegian society could undermine the reputation of Norway in international politics. These Norwegians are less willing to embrace diversity than one would expect from a country seeking to play the role of norm entrepreneur in world politics, whose leading politicians include global policy makers such as Fridtjof Nansen, Trygve Lie, and Gro Harlem Brundtland.

NOTES

1. Peter Lawler, "Scandinavian Exceptionalism and European Union," *The Journal of Common Market Studies* 34 (1997): 568.

2. See Erik Ringmar, "Re-Imagining Sweden: The Rhetorical Debate over EU Membership," *Scandinavian Journal of History* 23 (1998): 45–62.

3. See Gosta Esping-Andersen, *Politics against Markets* (Princeton, NJ: Princeton University Press, 1985), and the writings of Swedish political economist Jonas Pontusson.

4. See Oystein Sorensen, *Fridtjof Nansen: Mannen og myten* (Oslo: Universitetsforlaget, 1993), pp. 7–9.

5. Roland Huntford, *Nansen: The Explorer as Hero* (London: Gerald Duckworth and Company, 1997), p. 397.

6. Thorvald Stoltenberg, "Love of Man Is Practical Policy," *The Fridtjof Nansen Memorial Lectures* (Oslo: The Norwegian Academy of Science and Letters and the Norwegian Foreign Ministry, 1990), p. 65.

7. "Fridtjof Nansen: Statesman and Humanitarian," www.britannica.com.

8. "Fridtjof Nansen."

9. Speech by Fredrik Stang, chairman of the Nobel Committee, "The Nobel Prize for 1922," www.nobel.se/peace/laureates/1922/press.html, p. 1.

10. Stang, "The Nobel Prize for 1922," p. 3.

11. Stoltenberg, "Love of Man Is Practical Policy," p. 66.

12. Polish foreign minister Bronislaw Geremek, "Current Challenges for the OSCE and the Role of the Chairmanship" (Oslo: The Norwegian Atlantic Committee, Security Policy Library, #10, 1998), p. 20.

13. The history of Norwegian "bridge-building" is outlined in Johan Jorgen Holst (ed.), *Norwegian Foreign Policy in the 1980s* (Oslo: Norwegian University Press, 1985), and Nils Morten Udgaard, *Great Power Politics and Norwegian Foreign Policy* (Oslo: Norwegian University Press, 1973), pp. 125–130, 177.

14. Philip Burgess, *Elite Images and Foreign Policy Outcomes* (Columbus: Ohio State University Press, 1968), p. 82.

15. Burgess, *Elite Images and Foreign Policy Outcomes*, p. 82.

16. Udgaard, *Great Power Politics*, p. 125.

17. Udgaard, *Great Power Politics*, p. 148.

18. James Barros, *Trygve Lie and the Cold War: The UN Secretary-General Pursues Peace 1946–1953* (DeKalb: Northern Illinois University Press, 1989), p. 348.

19. Andrew Rigby, "Unofficial Nonviolent Intervention: Examples from the Israeli-Palestinian Conflict," *Journal of Peace Research* 32 (1995): 463.

20. Rigby, "Unofficial Nonviolent Intervention."

21. Avi Shlaim, "The Oslo Accord," *The Journal of Palestine Studies* 22 (Spring 1994): 25.

22. Jan Egeland, *Impotent Superpower—Potent Small State* (Oslo: Norwegian University Press, 1988).

23. David Satterfield, James Zogby, Ian Lustick, "Symposium: Reexamining the Arab-Israeli Peace Process," *Middle East Policy* 4 (1995).

24. Presentation by Thorvald Stoltenberg, at the Holst Symposium on Norwegian Foreign Policy, "Norway, Peace Negotiations, Human Rights: Effects and Influences," University of Washington, Seattle, October 24, 1996.

25. Johan Jorgen Holst, "Reflections on the Making of a Tenuous Peace, or the Transformation of Images of the Middle East Conflict," lecture presented at the School of International and Public Affairs, Columbia University, New York, September 28, 1993, pp. 4–5.

26. Holst, "Reflections on the Making of a Tenuous Peace," p. 5.

27. Daniel Lieberfeld, "Small Is Credible: Norway's Niche in International Dispute Settlement," *Negotiation Journal* 11, no. 3 (July 1995): 203.

28. Celia W. Dugger, "After Ferocious Fighting, Sri Lanka Struggles with Peace," *New York Times*, April 9, 2002, p. A6.

29. Interview with Jan Egeland in Lieberfeld, "Small Is Credible," p. 201.

30. "Norway Pledges Economic Support for Middle East Peace," *News of Norway* 50, no. 7 (October 1993): 1.

31. David Crystal, *The Cambridge Biographical Encyclopedia* (Cambridge: Cambridge University Press, 1994), pp. 151–152.

32. Thorbjorn Jagland, "On Norway and the European Defence Policy," speech to the Storting, June 9, 2000, Norwegian Foreign Ministry, Oslo.

33. Thomas Hylland Eriksen, "Globalization and Norwegian Identity," *Nytt fra Norge* (Oslo: Norwegian Ministry of Foreign Affairs, November 1996), p. 2.

34. "Bunad Ban Sparks Racism Charges," *Western Viking* 111, no. 40 (November 2000): 7.

35. "Modern Norway: Human Rights," *News of Norway* 57 (2000): 6.

36. "Modern Norway," p. 7.

37. See Dan Olweus, *Bullying at School: What We Know and What We Can Do* (Oxford, UK: Blackwell, 1993).

38. Frank Bruni, "A Nation that Exports Oil, Herring and Peace," *New York Times*, December 21, 2002.

· 5 ·

Globalists: Finland and Iceland

$\mathcal{T}$wo Scandinavian societies have repeatedly demonstrated toughness in the face of adversity and have challenged assumptions concerning the relative capacity of smaller powers in international politics. Finland and Iceland, the only two republics in Scandinavia, share a history of subordination and well-timed moves for independence from more powerful neighbors. These two societies gained their independence later than other Scandinavian states (Finland, 1917 and Iceland, 1944) and have developed distinct versions of social democratic institutions and practices. Both Finland and Iceland have generated exceptional wealth and standards of living for their small populations and have earned international reputations that defy their relative size.

Innovations in Finland and Iceland are impressive—for example, both governments sustain world-class national airlines, Finnair and Icelandair, which promote national cultural values via global transport. Visitors to Iceland may be surprised to find the preferential arrangements enjoyed by Icelandair, which enjoys a virtual monopoly at Keflavik Airport, outside of Reykjavik.

Security policy analysts puzzle over how Finland and Iceland have historically engaged powerful states in times of crisis. Against superior military strength, both Finland and Iceland have demonstrated steadfast resolve and commitment. And, in recent years, Finland and Iceland have broken free from the restraints of Cold War divisions to establish new agendas in the area of foreign-policy making—from Arctic cooperation agreements and recognition of the Baltic independence (Iceland) to active coordination with EU governments and acceptance of the euro (Finland). For these reasons, we refer to Finland and Iceland as globalists. These states and members of their societies counter the expectations of prominent theories of international relations. The

75

following analysis rejects the passive conception of Scandinavia implied by international relations theorists and illustrates how changes in global security and economic relations play out in two corners of Scandinavia—with surprising results.

DEFYING EXPECTATIONS: SMALL-STATE PROWESS

According to the expectations of prominent theories of international relations,

> small states have no significant armed forces and lack political or economic power. Small states are therefore suboptimal [vulnerable] from the point of view of security and face significant problems of existing in an unstable world of larger powers. This state of affairs leads to the question whether small states are independent in the same sense as larger states and whether their weakness prevents them from playing some part in the international community.[1]

Theories such as this, which focus on the material capacities of states, underestimate the importance of reputation in international politics. As Bjørn Olafsson argues in his study of Iceland in the global economy, "small states have the capacity to provide a high level of welfare for their citizens and function effectively in the international system."[2]

The Finns and Icelanders have, in critical moments, exercised extraordinary power as small states in world politics—beginning with their emergence as independent states.

NATIONAL INDEPENDENCE: GLOBAL OPPORTUNITIES

Finland and Iceland achieved their independence relatively late in comparison to the rest of Scandinavia. Formerly a part of the Swedish empire, Finland became an autonomous Russian Grand Duchy in 1809. The Russian Revolution provided an opportunity for Finnish nationalists to declare their independence in 1917. After a brief civil struggle, Finland consolidated its authority as an independent republic.

Iceland joined a union with Norway in 1262, consolidating its authority under the Norwegian king. When Denmark and Norway were united at the end of the fourteenth century, Iceland became a part of the Danish-Norwegian Union. During the sixteenth and seventeenth centuries, the Danes asserted greater control over Iceland—reforming domestic institutions, centralizing authority, and introducing a Danish monopoly trade regime.[3] Thus, the desire for independence gained momentum in the nineteenth century. In 1903, Denmark permitted Iceland to conduct its own domestic policy. During Denmark's occupation by Germany (1944), Icelanders declared their independence, and the country was recognized by the international community as a sovereign state.

In international security, Finns are well respected for standing up to the Soviets and incurring severe casualties against superior forces, while Iceland is notorious for firing shots at British trawlers to defend its decision to unilaterally extend the boundaries of its territorial waters and protect vital national fisheries. In the height of the Cold War, both Finland and Iceland offered their capitals as sites for building trust and forging cooperative agreements designed to dissipate conflict between the two opposing blocs. The Helsinki Accord and the Reykjavik Summit are examples of formative moments in the evolution of U.S.-Soviet relations. As participants in international markets, Finland has cultivated its role in trading with both East and West. Barter arrangements with the Soviet Union (Finnish goods traded for cheap energy) sustained the health of the Finnish economy and promoted its success as the "Japan of the North." The restructuring of Finland's leading forestry firm, Nokia, from a natural resource company to a global leader in the production of cellular phones represents another example of national ingenuity and skilled entrepreneurship. Iceland, on the other hand, is following a niche-market strategy as the largest producer of fishery gadgets in the world, and the government is actively seeking a reputation for Iceland in world politics by actively promoting research and development in alternative energy sources. Both countries exemplify resourcefulness in the face of limited resources and have pursued risky strategies in navigating relations with more powerful states in international relations.

INFERIOR FORCES, SURPRISING OUTCOMES

Despite Scandinavia's reputation as peace seekers, Finland and Iceland have battled for control over their territorial sovereignty against superior forces, with unexpected results. For the Finns, defending themselves against a more powerful neighbor was a difficult struggle, as documented in the film *Unknown Soldier* (produced by Toiva Särkkä, 1955).

The Soviet Union invaded Finland on November 30, 1939, and conflict between Finnish and Soviet forces continued until March 13, 1940. Initially, the Soviet Union sought to fully occupy and control Finnish territory. Finns became aware of Soviet intentions when Otto Kuusinen was established to head a puppet government in Karelia at the beginning of the war. However, the heavy casualties incurred by the Red Army led to a reassessment of strategy from rapid occupation to a war of attrition.[4] Finns prevented Russian advances, destroyed entire divisions, and even caused troops to retreat at particular moments in the conflict. Following the death of 200,000 men, approximately one million soldiers lost or wounded, and the destruction of a sizable number of Russian tanks, Stalin was willing to negotiate a settlement with the Finns.

The Finnish army developed an international reputation as tough, persistent fighters relying on techniques suited to the typography of the country. Skiing for miles in winter whites to a front, clearing an area and laying barbed wire, and throwing logs or grenades at oncoming enemy tanks are examples of unique Finnish fighting techniques, associated with what Finns call *sisu* or inner strength. Russian troops were poorly prepared for the particular terrain and temperatures they faced on the Finnish battlefield. Russians did not have adequate gear—nor were they able to supply heat for their units without lighting open fires. In contrast,

> no Finnish unit however small, is ever sent out upon operations of more than a few hours' duration without a source of heat perfectly adapted to its needs. . . . Finnish patrols, while their enemy fought against a temperature fifty below freezing, they lay underground, as comfortable as any hibernating animal, in dugouts lined with skins and roofed with birch logs supporting several feet of snow. In each of these dug-outs was a Finnish stove, designed to burn wood without a spark or a trace of smoke.[5]

Finnish fighting techniques are legendary and proudly retold to foreign visitors. For example, according to one account of fighting during the onset of the Winter War, "the Russians believed that fairly large forces of Finnish army were operating on all sides of them. But, in fact, there was nothing to oppose them but a patrol of sixty frontier guards, who raced on skis from position to position in order to give the impression that far larger numbers were hidden in the woods."[6] Superior skiing techniques and better battle equipment also permitted the Finns to outsmart superior numbers of Russian forces and inflict greater casualties than expected.

Finnish leaders have also been credited with *sisu*. Juho Kaarlo Paasikivi, Finland's second prime minister, allegedly called his government during a conversation with Stalin, "Will you please tell our 350,000 men that they will have to put three bullets in their rifles. The Russians say they could put a million men through Karelia if they wanted to." And when Stalin said, "I could send 10 million!" Paasikivi responded, "Alas! That's so many more for us to bury!"[7] Thus, Finns sustained a reputation for tough-mindedness in its encounters with a more powerful neighbor—even though the consequences of the Winter War changed the contours of the Finnish map.

By the spring of 1940, the Finns had lost substantial territory to the Soviets—including major parts of Karelia and a strip of land in the northern area of Finland. Yet, as Tomas Ries concludes, "the Peace Treaty cost Finland more than a settlement before the war would have done, but at the same time the war had forced Stalin to take a more careful look at the ability of Finland to defend her independence."[8]

In an opportunistic moment, Finns cooperated with the Germans in an effort to reclaim lost territory. Finland allowed German military divisions to pass through Finnish territory as part of Hitler's advance into northern Norway and the Soviet Union. In 1941, Finland mobilized the population for an attack on the Soviet Union and initiated the Continuation War (1941–1944). Finland sought to reclaim territories lost in the Winter War and never fully aligned with Germany. Although Finland failed to achieve its objectives, the postwar settlement enabled Finland to remain independent from the Soviet Union and avoid the fate of Central and Eastern Europe. Among the terms of the 1944 peace treaty, the Finns were required to pay $300,000 to the Soviet Union. They readily complied—without assistance from abroad. In contrast to the rest of Scandinavia, Finland did not accept any Marshall Plan assistance.

No Finn claims to have won either the Winter War or the War of Continuation. Yet the determination and fierce fighting of Finnish soldiers against the Russians provide an example of small-state prowess. Finland avoided inclusion in the Soviet bloc—even though vital territories were lost, and a military treaty signed in 1948 infringed on the capacity of the Finns to act independently in their foreign and security policies—until the break-up of the Soviet Union.

Finnish historian Tuomas Lehtonen refers to the outcome of Finland's two conflicts with the Soviet Union as "defensive victories," a term that also applies to Iceland's conflict over vital fishing areas in the 1970s.

SHOTS FIRED OVER FISH!

Iceland, with the smallest population size in Scandinavia, no independent military force, and an economy completely dependent on fishing, decided on three occasions to defend its vital resources from control by the British. Iceland and Britain engaged in three wars over control of cod fisheries: in

1958–1961, 1972–1973, and 1975–1976. As Jeffrey Hart argues, the British had superior military force, yet the outcome of these conflicts was highly favorable to the Icelanders.[9] Iceland's unilateral actions in the 1970s had two important consequences: New international legal agreements were reached that had broad implications for other small coastal states, and the British were restrained from accessing vital cod fisheries essential to Iceland's prosperity. Iceland utilized its membership in NATO and the strategic importance of the Keflavik NATO base as a means of seeking to resolve the conflict. Although democratic peace theorists maintain that democracies are less likely to go to war against one another, the Icelandic-British confrontations demonstrate the extent to which small, resource-dependent societies will go to protect precious resources against foreign control.

The first conflict between Iceland and Britain occurred in 1958, when the Icelandic government extended its fishery limits to twelve miles. According to Icelandic sources, the principal motivation for extending Icelandic control was the protection of fish stocks, based on the "Law Concerning the Scientific Conservation of the Continental Shelf Fisheries" of April 5, 1948. This regulation permitted the Ministry of Fisheries to issue regulations restricting fishing according to scientific research. According to Icelandic estimates, the stocks of cod and redfish were in decline.

From an Icelandic perspective, the government acted in accordance with widely accepted international legal regimes governing the high seas. The Icelandic decision followed the lead of developing nations (such as Ethiopia, Colombia, and the Dominican Republic) and entered into practice according to a 1958 Memorandum on Icelandic Fisheries submitted to the UN. Icelanders were practicing "sustainable development" before the term became codified in international development language. By extending its jurisdiction into the continental shelf, the government took legal action to prevent over fishing.

Principles of economic sovereignty and necessity justified Iceland's extension of its fishery limits: "The fisheries literally constitute a matter of life or death to the Icelandic people—for without them the country would not be habitable."[10] However, Britain failed to recognize Iceland's exclusive rights within these boundaries and permitted trawlers to enter these waters, under protection of the British navy. According to the 1958 report from the Icelandic Foreign Ministry ("British Aggression in Icelandic Waters"):

> The ignoble mission of these warships is to prevent the small Icelandic Coast Guard vessels from arresting British trawlers poaching within the limits. This they have done and are still doing by cutting off the Icelandic patrol boats from the trawlers and at times by ramming them and threat-

ening to sink them. . . . The Government of Iceland has repeatedly protested to the United Kingdom Government against this nefarious practice and demanded that the warships be immediately withdrawn from Icelandic waters . . . but all this has so far fallen on deaf British ears.[11]

In its report, the Foreign Ministry warned: "Serious incidents might occur at any time and the British warships should be withdrawn at once."[12] Seemingly fearless against superior might, the Icelanders refused to back down.

Iceland and Britain failed to resolve the dispute, and it flared up again in the 1970s. When a new Left-Agrarian coalition government announced its intent to unilaterally extend the fishery limits fifty miles off the coast of Iceland in July 1971, the decision (again) met with strong opposition by the British. The British government was neither consulted nor informed prior to the announcement, and a diplomatic exchange between London and Reykjavik ensued. Britain supported delaying such discussions until the Law of the Sea Conference convened in Chile in 1973. In defense of Iceland's position, Icelandic foreign minister Einar Agustsson held a press conference identifying the critical situation confronting Icelandic fisheries. According to the foreign minister, Icelandic fisheries were "threatened with imminent ruin" and "Iceland's fish were as much natural resources as were oil and gas, that 80 percent of Iceland's export revenue came from fish products, that the continental shelf was part of national territory, and that Iceland could not wait for the 1973 Law of the Sea Conference to formulate the rules on the fishery issue."[13] Subsequent statements by Icelandic prime minister Olafur Johannesson defended Iceland's decision to establish new fishery limits and represented a break with a 1961 fishery agreement between Britain and West Germany—the two largest participants in Icelandic fishing areas.[14]

The Icelanders presented the cod dispute as a crisis of resource management, with dire consequences for the nation if not resolved appropriately. The government openly blamed irresponsible fishery policies of larger industrial nations and defended the rights of a small island state to defend the exhaustible resources of the surrounding sea against overexploitation. Neither the Germans nor the British were able to reach a diplomatic solution and restore catch quotas with the Icelanders. Nor did Scandinavia's neighbors support the Icelandic position: Norwegians protested Iceland's decision as did the Swedes.

The British and the West Germans agreed to take the issue to the International Court of Justice (ICJ) for resolution. On August 17, 1972, the court decided to uphold the rights of annual catch limits for British and West German trawlers—even though the Icelanders questioned the jurisdiction of the court and maintained that the conditions had changed since the 1961 agreement on fishery catches rendering the deal null and void. The prime minister of Iceland announced the intent of the government to uphold the new fishery limits, acting against the decision of the ICJ.

On the day of the decision, approximately sixty or seventy British trawlers and ten or twenty West German trawlers sailed to Iceland in pursuit of cod. What ensued was an encounter, now famous in the study of international relations.

Iceland deployed its gunboats with hooks intended to destroy the wires of foreign trawlers. Icelanders also threatened to document all foreign vessels in territorial waters and to seek confrontation. Trawl wires of British vessels were cut—leading to a severe downturn in British-Icelandic relations. Icelandic vessels acted aggressively—firing blank shots across the bows of unwelcome vessels. The British trawlers called for the Royal Navy to intervene after additional wire-cutting incidents.

As the conflict continued, the British government agreed to send two frigates to the twelve- to fifty-mile zone. The Icelanders responded by banning Royal Air Force jets from access to the Keflavik base for refueling, and eventually extended the ban to all British aircraft.[15] The NATO Council became directly involved when both governments called on it to intervene. Recognizing the strategic importance of the NATO base, the Icelandic government also informed the United States of its intent to review the premises of the 1951 base agreement. As Jeffrey Hart puts it,

> Iceland had a lot to lose if its strategy did not work. The Keflavik base brought in $50–70 million per annum to the Icelandic economy; in 1973, this was around 4–8% of the gross national product. Trade with the North Atlantic nations would have dropped substantially if ties with NATO were cut. . . . But for the sake of protecting its fishery and increasing its share of the catch, Iceland was willing to risk imposing costs on itself and its NATO allies."[16]

Diplomatic activities intensified as the NATO base became linked to the fisheries dispute. Simultaneously, the preparations for the International Law of the Sea negotiations were underway, with a majority of governments endorsing a 200-mile economic zone in coastal waters. The British and Icelandic governments haggled over the size of catch limits and were unable to reach acceptable terms. Thus, another cod war occurred in 1975, which also resulted in shots fired at foreign trawlers.

International relations scholars (Joseph Nye and Jeffrey Hart) refer to the Icelandic-British confrontation as evidence of asymmetries in power relations and the possibilities for small states to emerge victorious because of a superior level of commitment. Engaging NATO and linking Iceland's base policy to the fisheries dispute heightened the pressure on the British government. The timing of the call for expanding the sovereignty of nations over coastal waters could not have been better for Iceland. In addition, the 1972 UN Conference on the Environment opened up a new era of global agenda setting, while the New International Economic Order and Law of the Sea discussions represented an opportunity for smaller economies to seek compensation in the world economy. By extending its jurisdiction into the seabed and justifying this measure internationally, Icelandic authorities helped codify the international legal norm now widely accepted: the exclusive economic zone. The following text was submitted to the Law of the Sea Conference Committee on April 5, 1973, by the Icelandic delegation: "A coastal state may determine the extent of its exclusive jurisdiction and control over natural resources of the maritime area adjacent to its territorial sea. The outer limits of this area shall be reasonable, keeping in view the geographical, geological, ecological, economic and other relevant local considerations, and shall not exceed 200 nautical miles."[17]

Did Icelanders have diplomatic connections through small-state networks that indicated the direction and substance of the Law of the Sea agenda? Or were they genuinely concerned over the depletion of cod stocks and consequences for Iceland's economy and society and served as "norm entrepreneurs" in extending this concept to the international community? Scholars and policy analysts continue to explore these questions to understand how and why the conflict could not be resolved diplomatically and the politics behind Icelandic actions.[18]

The legacy of the Finnish confrontations and Anglo-Icelandic Cod Wars are stunning examples of the power of the weak in international relations. The capacity for smaller states, relying on an "ideology of social partnership" (Katzenstein 1985) and mobilizing all possible resources to punch above their weight and successfully defend vital interests against larger, powerful states in the international system, is demonstrated in these case studies.

The reputation of Finland and Iceland as fierce competitors also extends to the marketplace. The transformation of Nokia, Finland's leading hi-tech company, and the willingness of Icelanders to embrace new technologies have made these countries prosperous and internationally well known.

EMBRACING TECHNOLOGY

Finland currently holds a leading position in the global production of mobile phones. Nokia is internationally recognized as a competitive player in the production of cell phones. In recent years, the company has aggressively pursued new markets—including the sale of wireless phones to China. Product placement (from advertisements to films) and Nokia's sponsorship of international athletic events have elevated attention to the products and image of the Finnish company.

Nokia has a long, distinguished history in Finland as a producer of forestry products. Finland's economic prosperity relied on the export of pulp and paper products to foreign markets. The Nokia forestry company was founded in the 1860s and began evolving into a technology firm one hundred years later. The forestry company relied on mobile phones to communicate and gradually moved its entire operation into electronics.

By the 1990s

> the Nokia mobile telephone handset became the leading high-tech consumer product manufactured in Finland. The Finns' fascination with technical innovations already caught the attention of foreign observers in the nineteenth century. It has been suggested that enthusiasm for technical equipment is typical of "pioneering cultures." In this respect, Finland and the other Nordic countries have a closer affinity with the American frontier mentality than they do with, say, southern Europe.[19]

Nokia has surpassed Ericsson (Sweden) in the sale of mobile phones—even though Finland's economy is half the size of its neighbor. Ericsson, as a consequence, may seek to relinquish market shares to Nokia and other competitors and move into the production of satellite technology.

Size, it seems, is not an obstacle to entrepreneurship, as a further example from Iceland demonstrates. Iceland is one of the most technologically advanced societies in the world today. The information technology (IT) sector is growing rapidly, and Icelanders are heavy users of cell phones (80 percent) and the Internet (70 percent). Approximately 40 percent of all transactions in Iceland are conducted electronically.[20] Although Iceland still depends heavily on traditional economic activities (fishing, aluminum smelting, and tourism), the society is relying more heavily on IT, telecommunications, and software—a change facilitated by the Icelandic government. So, for example, fish catches are recorded by sophisticated software, and Iceland's websites promote its national culture and tourist activities.

The conservative Independence Party is the predominant player in Icelandic politics and has aggressively promoted privatization, restructuring, lower tariffs on hi-tech imports, increased foreign investment, and other innovations. One example of the government's promotion of new technologies is the recent policy to grant Icelanders full access to scientific journals available over the Internet. This policy is designed to improve the skills and knowledge of the Icelandic workforce and is the first of its kind internationally. In addition, Iceland's national university (the University of Iceland, located in the capital city of Reykjavik) actively seeks partnerships with foreign universities and has recently restructured its course offerings to appeal to international students.

Another Icelandic initiative seeks to place Iceland at the leading edge of new energy technologies. The government plans to move toward a carbon-free economy, relying on hydrogen fuel cell technology. Iceland's primary energy requirements come from abundant hydroelectric power and geothermal energy sources. To create a new, clean energy source and move the economy away from dependence on fossil fuels, the Icelandic government announced a new initiative to separate hydrogen and oxygen from water. Hydrogen will be used to provide fuel cells for Icelandic buses, with substantial investment (6.4 million U.S. dollars) from Daimler Chrysler, Royal Dutch/Shell Group, and the EU. In 1990, the hydrogen fuel cell technology was too expensive to attract investment. However, according to a leading expert, Bragi Arnason, professor of chemistry, University of Iceland, the cost of producing fuel cells has decreased. Innovations permit scientists to produce methanol from hydrogen and carbon dioxide, necessary to provide fuel cells for automobiles, trucks, and ships. In the future, according to Arnason, Iceland may become a net exporter of energy, or the "Kuwait of the north."[21]

Not all of the initiatives of the Icelandic government have been widely supported. In an effort to pursue foreign investment, new partnerships have been forged with international companies to expand aluminum-smelting activities. To attract investment and build the largest industrial plant in Iceland, vital wilderness areas will be adversely affected. Construction of a hydroelectric dam threatens to flood a protected wilderness area north of Vatnajokull Glacier. Numerous environmental studies have been conducted concerning this project, with disturbing results. Political controversy and social protests surround this effort by the government of Prime Minister David Oddson to internationalize the economy and reduce dependence on fisheries. If the government wins this fight, it will bring more jobs to eastern Iceland. Foreign partners (such as Alcoa) find this project attractive because of the relatively low energy costs available in Iceland from abundant dams and geothermal sources. However, the controversy could jeopardize Iceland's reputation as an international leader in ecologically sound development practices.

GLOBAL STRATEGIES FOR NORM ENTREPRENEURSHIP

Nonetheless, the economies of both Finland and Iceland have cultivated a position in international markets as technologically advanced societies with competitive capacities that continue to outpace other societies. The willingness to embrace global change and make opportunities out of limited resources is a legacy of all the Nordic societies—yet by the 1990s, Finland and Iceland surged ahead of petrol-dependent Norway, economic crisis–ridden Sweden, and the original leader in niche markets, the Danes.

In relations with their largest export market (the EU), Finland and Iceland have followed entirely different paths. Finland resisted joining the EU, preferring looser partnerships during the Cold War era. However, the breakup of the Soviet Union and economic crisis in Finland led to a redirection of foreign policy. Finns joined the EU with Sweden and Austria on January 1, 1995. Since their entry, they have played a decisive role in strengthening integration initiatives and became the first Scandinavian government to enter the euro zone.

Iceland, on the other hand, remains aloof from EU institutions. The leading political parties are skeptical about embedding the society in a regional governance system that has a less conservationist fisheries policy than Iceland has. For example, the Common Fisheries Policy, or "Blue Europe," is not as restrictive as Iceland's regime, yet fish account for 70 percent of Icelandic exports. Icelanders "worry that European investors could take over local land and business, even the choicest salmon rivers. Economic arguments for membership fail to impress . . . and the country enjoys one of the highest standards of living in the world."[22]

For some northern Europeans, formal cooperation with other European governments is a necessity. The possibility of influencing the direction and substance of European cooperation is attractive. For other northern Europeans, remaining outside the formal channels of European governance is required to protect national interests. Finland and Iceland represent two opposite strategies and different visions of European unity in their foreign relations.

As this chapter argues, the memories of Finland's fierce defense of its sovereignty in the Winter War and War of Continuation and Iceland's determined defense of its establishment of an Exclusive Economic Zone to protect their vital fisheries significantly enhance their reputations as principled actors in international relations—willing to challenge opponents and to rely on innovative strategies against superior might. Consider how other measures by Scandinavians have contributed to establishing new norms in the international system and strengthening international regimes—defying experts who discount the limited capacities of smaller powers. The following chapter explores how these societies build new initiatives and establish codes of appropriate behavior in world politics.

NOTES

1. Bjorn Olafsson, *Small States in the Global System* (Aldeshot, UK: Ashgate Publishers, 1998), p. 48.

2. Olafsson, *Small States in the Global System*, p. 155.

3. Ragnar Arnason, *The Icelandic Fisheries* (Oxford, UK: Fishing News Books, 1995), p. 11.

4. Tuomas Lehtonen, *Europe's Northern Frontier: Perspectives on Finland's Western Identity* (Porvoo, Finland: Finnish National Fund for Research and Development, 1999), p. 98; Tomas Ries, *Cold Will: The Defence of Finland* (London: Brassey's Defence Publishers, 1988), pp. 82–83.

5. John Langdon-Davies, *Invasion in the Snow* (Boston: Houghton Mifflin Company, 1941), p. 17.

6. Langdon-Davies, *Invasion in the Snow*, p. 11.

7. Herbert B. Elliston, *Finland Fights* (Boston: Little, Brown and Company, 1940), p. 142.

8. Ries, *Cold Will*, p. 84.

9. Jeffrey Hart, *The Anglo-Icelandic Cod War of 1972–1973: A Case Study of a Fishery Dispute* (Berkeley: Institute of International Studies, University of California, 1976), pp. 1–4.

10. Iceland Ministry of Foreign Affairs, *British Aggression in Icelandic Waters* (Reykjavik: June 1959), p. 17.

11. Iceland Ministry of Foreign Affairs, *British Aggression in Icelandic Waters*, p. 5.

12. Iceland Ministry of Foreign Affairs, *British Aggression in Icelandic Waters*, p. 23.

13. Hart, *The Anglo-Icelandic Cod War*, p. 7.

14. See Johannes Nordal and Valdimar Kristinsson, *Iceland: 874–1974* (Reykjavik: The Central Bank of Iceland, 1975), p. 194.

15. Hart, *The Anglo-Icelandic Cod War*, p. 39.

16. Hart, *The Anglo-Icelandic Cod War*, p. 43.

17. Nordal and Kristinsson, *Iceland: 874–1974*, p. 172.

18. Morris Davis, *Iceland Extends Its Fisheries Limits: A Political Analysis* (Oslo: Universitetsforlaget, 1963).

19. Lehtonen, *Europe's Northern Frontier*, p. 55.

20. Adam Rombel, "Island Nation Rides the Tech Tides," *Global Finance* 16, no. 10 (October 2002).

21. "Iceland Plans Carbon-Free Economy," *Chemical and Engineering News*, vol. 79, August 13, 2001, and discussions with Icelandic expert, Ted Beck, University of Washington, Seattle, November 22, 2002.

22. "Odd Man Out under Oddson," *The Economist*, March 14, 1992, p. 56.

· 6 ·

Risks to Scandinavia's Reputation

$\mathcal{A}$s Scandinavian societies assert themselves on the global stage, from the promotion of peace, human rights, social justice, gender equality, and environmentalism, there are paradoxes at home that pose a threat to Scandinavia's image and reputation abroad. One of the most serious challenges to the survival of Scandinavia's universal system of welfare capitalism is its capacity to accept and tolerate difference. In the 1950s, intra-Nordic migration accounted for diversity within the societies (Finns to Sweden; Norwegians to Denmark, etc.). However, fifty years later, 10 percent of the population in the major cities in Scandinavia are immigrants whose countries of origin include Sri Lanka, Turkey, Sudan, Ethiopia, Iran, Yugoslavia, and Iraq. Media images and popular perceptions associate immigration with higher incidences of crime in Scandinavian societies. Equal treatment of new populations engage principles of human rights and social justice *within* Scandinavian politics, with populist parties supporting more restrictive approaches than expected by those who study this corner of Europe.

Providing a safe haven for refugees and those in need of poverty assistance and/or human rights protection is a cornerstone of the Scandinavian model. Yet integration and assimilation within these societies has proven difficult.[1] Diversification and integration of new groups has also coincided with socioeconomic changes, further compounding the challenges for Scandinavian societies.

Diversification of Scandinavia has raised issues of class, race, and identity that are new sources of tension and politicization within these relatively homogeneous societies. The predominant ethnic division within northern European countries is the Sami people, a nomadic population residing above the Arctic Circle extending from Norway into Sweden, Finland, and Russia.

In contrast to other European states such as France, Britain, or the Netherlands, Scandinavians were not heavily engaged in acquisition of colonies, nor did these countries experience the influx of immigrants associated with empire. Instead, Scandinavia was historically a net exporter of immigrants who traveled by ship to North America in search of better living conditions. Even though the idea of emigration is fundamental to Scandinavia's historical development, the growing numbers of increasingly diverse populations of immigrants pose a unique challenge to the Scandinavian model. The political challenge of immigration has intensified since the 1970s and has led international observers (and Scandinavians themselves) to question the premises of the welfare model that is founded on principles of equality, social justice, and fundamental human rights—for *all* members of society.

Who immigrates to Scandinavia and why? Immigration to Scandinavia may be differentiated according to several categories. These include temporary workers and seasonal labor, asylum seekers or refugees, individuals born outside Scandinavia relocating for work or family purposes, and illegal immigrants. Scandinavia is relatively affluent in the world economy and has established policies and programs designed to combat poverty and inequality. In recent decades, the number of immigrants to Scandinavia has grown considerably, particularly in the early 1990s with the collapse of the Soviet Union and relocation of peoples from former Yugoslavia.

New debates have ensued over the appropriate ways to accommodate incoming populations. Scandinavians disagree over how to ethically and morally take care of new populations. Should the immigrants be required to learn the host language? If political, economic, and social conditions improve in the country from which a refugee or asylum seeker has migrated, should the individual and his or her family be repatriated at the expense of the host country? Will the costs of inclusion overwhelm the resources of an already burdened welfare state? Are immigrants contributing to the economic welfare of the nation? Should diverse populations be encouraged to maintain their own cultural, linguistic, and religious practices?

Immigrants come to Scandinavia from a diversity of countries of origin and vary in total numbers. Patterns of immigration also reflect zones of poverty in the world economy and areas where human rights violations, ethnic unrest, or the break-up of the state has occurred. Icelandic immigration is predominantly from Asia, and Iceland is only beginning to discuss the transition to multiculturalism because (as in Finland) this is a relatively new socioeconomic development. In Sweden, with the largest total number of immigrants, and in Denmark and Norway there are more immigrants from former Yugoslavia, Turkey, and Iraq, and a growing number of immigrants from Africa. The majority of Finland's immigrant population is from the former Soviet Union, with smaller numbers of immigrants from the former Yugoslavia, Iran, and Turkey. The influx of larger numbers of immigrants from increasingly diverse parts of the world coincided with global economic changes that have exacerbated the challenges associated with assimilating "the other" in these societies. Patterns of immigration to Scandinavia are provided in table 6.1 and table 6.2.

Table 6.1.   Residents from Non-western Countries Living in Sweden and Denmark

	2001		
Sweden		*Denmark*	
Former Yugoslavia	73,274	Turkey	29,680
Iraq	55,696	Bosnia-Herzegovina	18,027
Bosnia-Herzegovina	52,198	Iraq	15,099
Syria	14,646	Pakistan	10,313

Source: Excerpts from table 1, UNU/WIDER. "A Tale of Two Countries: Poverty Among Immigrants in Denmark and Sweden Since 1984." Discussion Paper No. 2003/36, April 2003, p. 8.

Table 6.2.   Largest Groups of Non-western Foreign Nationals in Norway

	2001
Bosnia and Herzegovina	11,611
Iraq	9,891
Pakistan	6,731
Somalia	6,152

Source: Statistics Norway, "Trends of Migration to and from Norway and the Situation of Immigrants in Norway," November 2003, p. 18.

IMMIGRATION TO SCANDINAVIA: GLOBALIZATION AT HOME

The international oil crises of the 1970s elevated the costs of production and introduced more competitive conditions for Scandinavian exports. Scandinavian manufacturers lost market shares in important sectors—from Swedish automobile production to Danish agricultural trade. While traditionally viewed as model societies because of the low levels of unemployment (between 1 and 3 percent), Scandinavia today experiences higher levels of unemployment, with some societies closer to the European average of approximately 10 percent of the labor force without jobs. During periods of Scandinavian labor shortages, governments encouraged immigrants to participate in the labor market. For example, as Norway developed its international oil sector in the 1970s, the economy relied heavily on imported labor. However, by the 1990s, growing competition for jobs placed new pressures on Scandinavian welfare states as more people sought support and found it difficult to find work.

It has been difficult for new groups to contribute to the domestic economy and assimilate in Scandinavian society. According to a 1996 report by the Swedish government,

> the labor-market marginalization of many with an immigrant background and the consequent growing dependence on welfare payments is both a social and an economic problem . . . the motive [for proposing some labor-market policy measures differentially treating migrants] is that the employment gap between them and others is so great that it risks making permanent welfare dependents of so many.[2]

Comparative studies of immigration confirm these trends. For example, the UN University World Institute for Development Economics Research Institute concluded the following: between 1980 and 2003, more and more immigrants in Denmark and Sweden are from less-developed countries, and "the difference in poverty rates between natives and immigrants has grown."[3] In Finland, the increasing number of immigrants has corresponded to a similar disparity in patterns of unemployment. Unemployment is markedly higher among foreign-born residents than it is among the rest of the population. Critics such as Olavi Koivukangas, from the Institute of Migration in Turku, Finland, attribute differences in employment levels to "xenophobia and negative attitudes."[4] In 2004, new measures were taken by the Finnish government to counter negative attitudes toward immigrants and to point to the positive influence of immigrants in the labor force as the country faces a labor shortage. Similar efforts have been made in Norway, as government studies are introduced indicating the positive economic effects of immigrant labor.

The risks to the Scandinavian model are, in our assessment, aggravated by the stigma now associated with a marginalized labor pool of immigrant background. If members of these societies cannot identify themselves as one group, unified around common ideas of nation, or accept multiple identities within the nation, it is problematic for the norms of universalism essential to the cradle-to-grave model of welfare capitalism to persist. For, as Eric Einhorn and John Logue argue, the problem is not only economic, but cultural:

> The sudden appearance of significant groups with very different cultural norms in the midst of your neighborhood—who worshiped differently, who saw themselves as distinctive, who slaughtered their animals differ-

ently, and occasionally slaughtered their daughters as well when they "shamed the family" by rejecting arranged marriages—strains social bonds.[5]

As Scandinavia becomes more multicultural, the fundamental norm of universalism is at stake. To ensure the health of a system based on the principle of equal access to benefits for all members of society, there must be a society-wide understanding of belonging. Some scholars, such as Peter Katzenstein, refer to this as an ideology of social partnership. If divisions emerge over "we" versus "them," and the culture is unable to redefine its traditions and day-to-day practices to accommodate differences and translate these into membership, the model of Scandinavian welfare is at risk.

For scholars who study Scandinavia, the multicultural transformation and globalization occurring *within* Scandinavia is both a fascinating and a promising liberalization of strict social norms (introducing new ideas, flavors, traditions, dress codes, types of entertainment, and variety to complement *lefsa, lutefisk, bunads,* Bergman film festivals, and aquavit) and a potentially destabilizing force, driving Scandinavia to undermine its own version of exceptionalism and to be internationally reprimanded for failing to apply principles of human rights advocated abroad to those residing at home.

To be foreign or "*fremmed*" in the Scandinavian cultural context is to be different. And Scandinavia has championed a position *against* the idea of difference in its moral views of how others should act. Thus, during the 1960s, the United States was heavily criticized by prominent Scandinavians, including Gunnar Myrdal, for discrimination and civil rights abuses. More recently, the system of apartheid in South Africa was considered morally unacceptable.[6] Yet, within Scandinavian societies, a process is underway that divides these societies between those who are included in the majority population and those who coexist in the same society yet are segregated economically, politically, socially, and within the education system.

As Scandinavian societies engage more diverse populations, the understanding of how institutions, policies, and collective identities are transformed is subject to critical review. The classic social science approaches to the study of Scandinavia explain the model according to enduring institutional relationships, from the power of labor in society (Esping-Andersen 1985) ; and the historic compromises of the 1930s based on principles of social partnership (Katzenstein 1985); to the novel policies and programs implemented in northern Europe (Einhorn and Logue 2003).

Jonas Pontusson, on the other hand, anticipated a weakening of social democracy in Sweden as a consequence of a more divided labor force. For Pontusson, the emergence of a new class of white-collar workers with

separate organizations and interests created divisions within the labor movement.[7] A similar analysis can be made of the more diverse and segregated labor force emerging in Scandinavia today. The new division within Scandinavian society is a more segregated labor force as a consequence of growing
diversity in these societies. The challenge is further complicated by patterns
of employment and exclusion from the labor market among immigrant populations. Unless identities are redefined, these developments suggest a weakening of the ideology of social partnership, one of the defining features of
Scandinavian democratic corporatism outlined by Katzenstein.

Optimistic expectations for the survival and resilience of the Scandinavian model are championed in Sweden, where the government has a lengthy
experience of reaching out to multicultural groups since the 1960s. One of the
leading scholars of the welfare state, Bo Rothstein, predicts the continuation
of universal welfare norms despite growing diversity and tension within Sweden over how the system should be reformed. In fact, calls for reform, for
Rothstein, are evidence that the system itself is responsive and adaptive.
However, there are other, less constructive strategies currently under implementation that could preserve the universal welfare system, and, at the same
time, endanger the progressive image of Scandinavia in world politics. Consider the evolution of Scandinavian immigration policies and the paradox of
anti-immigrant developments in a global age.

The most critical assessment of Sweden's immigration policy is written
by Allan Pred, a non-Swede, and entitled *Even in Sweden.* The author documents numerous incidents of discrimination and racism that contradict the
expectations held within the society and by outsiders of the openness and pro-
gressiveness of Scandinavian societies—particularly Sweden, which has cultivated this image heavily in its cultural policies. And although the Swedish
government embraced multiculturalism earlier, it has its own legacy to con-
tend with today. A Swedish housing policy, designed to create an international living arrangement for non-Swedes, has ghettoized particular ethnic
groups in areas outside the inner cities. Even when the policy is unintentional
(as in Norway), certain areas of Oslo are designated zones of diversity where
restaurants, markets, and ethnic enclaves are more likely to be found. In Denmark, crossing the block from one side of the street to another in Copenhagen
can mean the difference between one world and another. Ethnic Russians in
Finland co-mix with Finns yet may be viewed differently outside Helsinki, in
the northern areas.

If Swedish social scientist Bo Rothstein's predictions hold, the Scandinavian model of universal social policy will evolve to meet the requirements
of a new set of demands, as is typical of democratic institutions. However, if
sociologist Allan Pred is correct, the ethnic and racial segregation of societies

will undermine Scandinavian ideals of justice and equality. In this analysis, the risks pose not just a domestic crisis, but also have important international repercussions for Scandinavia's capacity to play a global role.

Another risk to Scandinavia's reputation is the decline of trust at home. There is a growing perception in Scandinavia today that the incidence of crime is on the rise, and the cause is associated with globalism (i.e., people who were not born there and/or are connected to international crime syndicates). Mrs. Palme attributed the murder of her husband Olof Palme to a down-and-out Stockholmer, but some observers attribute Palme's death to Sweden's international engagement in the trade of arms. The murderer of Swedish foreign minister Anna Lindh was unstable with a demonstrated record of violence and international connections to the former Yugoslavia. Norway's national treasure, *The Scream*, painted by Edvard Munch, was stolen on two occasions, with much suspicion surrounding possible connections abroad. The assumption of guilt or innocence does not appear to be evenly distributed as Scandinavia confronts common challenges facing other advanced industrial societies. "*Utlendinger*," or "people out of the land," can and do complain of unfair or unequal treatment—both subtle and deliberate. Media images perpetuate a sense of distrust of newcomers who are less likely to respect the local traditions, laws, and rules so important in Scandinavian societies.

The exclusive social networks contribute to a sense of isolation among noncitizens. Even if individuals have lived in Scandinavia for their entire lives, they may be left off an invitation to a social event because they did not attend the same kindergarten class or sewing club. The barriers to entry in Scandinavian society and culture have always been high, and without generations of engagement, it may be difficult (if not impossible) to fully participate in the cultural life of these societies. Hence, a growing separatism is visible in the inner cities and surrounding areas, complicated by a blurring of difference as Swedes and Africans, Norwegians and Hungarians, and Somalis and Danes intermarry and create a new generation of multicultural Scandinavians.

A significant contribution to national discussion(s) of difference and diversity is occurring in the literature and film of contemporary Scandinavia. Writers such as Henning Mankell and filmmakers born outside the area are introducing important cultural artifacts and raising critical questions in these societies. In the Swedish context, the contribution of literary critics to a serious self-evaluation of exceptionalism and egalitarianism is a productive engagement, which leaves many observers optimistic about the promise of integrating new groups into society. One of the most popular films in Sweden portrays a stereotypical Volvo-driving citizen who encounters an exotic, dynamic immigrant family. The humor, derived from a portrayal of distinct cultures living side by side within the same society, has a healing quality that gives promise to an emerging idea of multiculturalism. Thus, the Swedes appear to be engaging the social challenges of difference directly, in recent contributions to popular culture and literature.

In other ways, though, the transformation of societies from homogeneous to multicultural appears to be proceeding less progressively. For example, the publications circulated by the Swedish Immigration Board's Information Division in the 1980s provided advice to immigrants on how to fit in to Swedish society. However, by reproducing images of a society without incorporating difference into the profile or history of nation, there was no prescription for inclusion into Swedish society. Instead, foreigners need to tolerate the way Swedes treat each other and not expect too much. The advice to immigrants included: learn the Swedish language; respect and accept Swedish traditions; keep your own identity; and do your best to fit in. In one publication, the recommendations to immigrants have included unwritten codes of conduct:

> You do not usually drop in on people in Sweden, at least not in towns and cities. The Swedes hate to intrude, they respect each other's privacy. For this reason, they do not invite the neighbors in for quite some time. . . . You can try inviting your Swedish neighbors in for coffee, for your national dish or to visit your club. Some of them will decline because they will feel unable to cope with a foreign language and different habits.[8]

Where is the manual for Swedes, advising them on how to become multicultural? There are contradictions, as one population engages another. Government authorities pronounce the end of difference and offer inspiring billboards discouraging racism and encouraging tolerance. Yet societal attitudes are slow to change, leading to discouragement and misunderstandings. In the words of one immigrant, "It upsets me to see people kissing in the street. Why do they have to make such a show?" Another said, "I do not feel the slightest bit Swedish and never will. I feel like the eternal stranger who is always homesick."[9] Scandinavians have engaged the racism issue directly—in progressive and regressive ways.

In 2004, the Nobel Peace Prize was awarded to the first African woman in history, demonstrating to the international community the importance of affirming environmental agendas, gender, and difference. Ironically, however, the prospect for an African woman to live, work, and culturally engage as an equal within the Scandinavian political culture remains a severe challenge. The rights and responsibilities of immigrants have become politically contested in Denmark and subject to international scrutiny as more restrictive policies are put in place that endanger the progressive image of Danishness.

DENMARK RESTRICTS IMMIGRANT LABOR

Immigration has become increasingly politicized throughout Scandinavia in recent decades. Each of the political parties includes one or more references to the role of immigrants in society on its official platform. And as the number of immigrants continues to grow, the public and the political sphere debate the appropriate ways to integrate new groups into northern Europe's relatively homogeneous societies. Welfare state reform and a growing perception that if Denmark expands cooperation with other European governments in the EU more and more foreigners will come have exacerbated an already tense situation at home.

Scandinavia's reputation as peaceful, progressive, and tolerant is susceptible to reevaluation, as incidences of ethnic-related violence capture media attention. As Danish expert Lisa Togeby explains in *Fremmedhed og Fremmedhad i Danmark*, following the 1985 decision to place sixty Iranians in the city of Kalundborg, a group of several hundred Danes demonstrated against the presence of *de fremmede* by destroying the windows with bottles and demanding entry into their living facility. Attitudes toward the Iranians reported in the press were decidedly intolerant, mentioning the propensity of Iranians to use knives and to receive more social assistance than the Danes themselves had access to.[10] Togeby's interviews conducted in 1993 revealed negative attitudes toward immigrants from economic, social welfare, cultural, and racial perspectives. Stereotypes of immigrants abound, from media images to political cartoons.

Following the November 1991 election, the Conservative-Right coalition government introduced a more restrictive approach to immigration. A new policy limited the capacity of immigrants to bring spouses to the country by introducing age restrictions and requiring proof of monetary support. In 1998, the adoption of the Danish Act on Integration of Aliens introduced a new quota system, distributing refugees around the country according to geographic measures of equality. For Togeby, the government's response has been inadequate and in some cases inappropriate (as in the decision to send immigrants back where they came from as advocated by the Progress Party leader Helge Dohrmann), suggesting the need for moral leadership to counter ethnocentric tendencies in Danish society. As one observer put it, "the lack of social contacts between foreigners and Danes [has created] a 'lagoon of ignorance' with prejudices, fears and xenophobic feelings . . . leading to an intensified perception of foreigners as a threat to the existing social system."[11]

The debate over immigration continues to divide Danes and to attract international scrutiny. The EU and the UN have issued reports critical of developments in Danish immigration policy. In addition, media accounts accentuate divisions within the society over appropriate assimilation strategies. Accusations of racism and national exclusion have been soundly rejected by Danish politicians. Nonetheless, the reputation of progressive Danes has been severely challenged in the international community.

Ethnic minorities are underrepresented politically in Denmark and excluded from important social networks. Danes themselves are concerned about these matters and have been introducing new anti-discrimination and anti-racism measures to impose zero-tolerance norms from above. Traditional ways of organizing, such as membership in soccer clubs, are engaging a multicultural Denmark—with some evidence(s) of success as new participants are recruited and inclusion is celebrated.[12]

Other Scandinavian societies are engaging the immigration question, with several notable patterns. Political parties with pro- and anti-immigration platforms are more visibly a part of national politics than in previous decades. Immigrants are both more willing to do the jobs Scandinavians resist (late-night shopkeepers, taxi drivers, and tram operators), contributing to a new underclass within these societies. Immigrants to Finland include educated Russians and Estonians, yet many entered the country in the 1990s during the worst unemployment crisis in Finnish history and have experienced discrimination and hostility, according to the Institute of Migration.[13] Icelanders have the fewest number of immigrants and are only beginning to discuss issues of assimilation, integration, and human rights that have been discussed earnestly elsewhere in Scandinavia for several decades.

European integration and EU membership provide another level of governance for Finland, Sweden, and Denmark that also have implications for how these societies engage new populations. In 1995, the EU incorporated fair treatment of immigrants in a measure designed to counter racism and xenophobia in EU member-states.

A redefinition of Scandinavianism is underway, with consequences for the global role and legitimacy of these societies. And, as in other national contexts, it is important to document what aspects of a nation's past is included and what is excluded. The act of writing a national history of the immigrant experience is an effort to include difference as part of memory. Norwegians introduced a new national history of immigration in 2003, authored by Hallvard Tjelmeland and Grete Brochmann. Through these efforts, Scandinavian multiculturalism is evolving.

If Bo Rothstein's predictions are correct, the Scandinavian model will continue to adapt from within, incorporating new groups and retaining a commitment through solidarity to a universal provision of welfare policies. However, should the prospect of assimilating larger numbers of diverse populations become too great, there could be an institutional change in the organization and delivery of social policies precisely because the society no longer views itself as one nation and one class. If, collectively, the project of inclusion fails, the predictions made by Jonas Pontusson regarding a weakening of social democracy may result—for reasons unanticipated by earlier theorizing. And if there is contradiction between modes of engaging the international polity and the ways difference is practiced at home, Scandinavia's reputation can and will be in jeopardy. This is more of a warning than a prediction, acknowledging the separate ways in which government, society, economy, and the universal welfare state interact with immigrant populations in Iceland, Denmark, Norway, Sweden, and Finland.

The final chapter identifies Scandinavia's legacy in world politics and the enduring ways norm entrepreneurship persists, even against tremendous domestic and international transformations.

NOTES

1. Allan Pred, *Even in Sweden: Racisms, Racialized Spaces and the Popular Geographical Imagination* (Berkeley: University of California Press, 2000).

2. Statens offentliga utredningar, 1996, cited in Pred, *Even in Sweden*, p. 163.

3. UNU/WIDER, "A Tale of Two Countries: Poverty among Immigrants in Denmark and Sweden since 1984," Discussion Paper No. 2003/36, April 2003, p. 19.

4. Olavi Koivukangas, "Foreigners in Finland," *Politics and Society*, Virtual Finland. virtual.finland.ni/netcomm/news/showarticle.asp?intNWSAID=25787. Accessed November 28, 2005.

5. Eric Einhorn and John Logue, *Modern Welfare States: Scandinavian Politics and Policy in the Global Age* (Westport, CT: Praeger, 2003), p. 312.

6. Peter Nannestad, *Solidaritetens Pris: Holdningen til indvandrere og flygtninge I Denmark 1987–1993* (Aarhus, Denmark: Aarhus Universitetsforlag, 1999), pp. 16–17.

7. Jonas Pontusson, *The Limits of Social Democracy: Investment Politics in Sweden* (Ithaca, NY: Cornell University Press, 1992).

8. Swedish Immigration Board, *Sweden: A General Introduction for Immigrants* (Varnamo, Sweden: AB Falths Tryckeri, 1989), pp. 12–13.

9. Swedish Immigration Board, *Sweden*, p. 8.

10. Lise Togeby, *Fremmedhed og Fremmedhad i Danmark* (Copenhagen, Denmark: Columbus, 1997), p. 9.

11. Jan Hjarno, "Causes of the Increase in Xenophobia in Denmark," manuscript, 1993, cited in Maria Gulicova-Grethe, "Intpol—Denmark: The Politics of Adaptation and Integration in Denmark," manuscript, 1993, p. 2.

12. Bronshoj Boldklub is cited as an example of ethnic inclusion (80 percent of the youth are minorities) by Gulicova-Grethe, "Intpol—Denmark," p. 24.

13. Finnish Institute of Migration. www.migrationinstitute.fi/db/articles/art.php?artid=34. Accessed November 28, 2005.

· 7 ·

Conclusion: The New Scandinavian Way

$\mathcal{O}$utsiders see Scandinavia as a benign player in international politics, with a prominent presence in building international institutions, tirelessly promoting a collective vision of how power *should* be exercised in world politics. As one observer put it, "five small states, comprising eight small nations, on the edge of the inhabitable world have somehow managed to create independent, free, prosperous societies, dedicated to justice in social affairs and tolerant of all shades of opinion—states that coexist in peace."[1]

Scandinavia has always been connected to other parts of the globe— from the Viking age to the Internet era. And, as Peter Katzenstein and other leading scholars have argued, it is continually required to adjust to changes in the international system. Yet new imperatives position Scandinavia to play a critical role in how the international system evolves. Even though the height of Scandinavian social democracy and the "third way" between socialism and capitalism no longer capture the essence of life in the north, governments and leading members of these societies are still seeking to (re)structure the international agenda. And in many areas, such as the environment, global aid policy, conflict resolution, gender equality, and human rights, their longstanding practices give them greater legitimacy to play a global role than more powerful states such as the United States.

For many international relations scholars, Scandinavia is a marginal, seemingly unimportant corner of Europe whose role in the system is conditioned and defined by larger powers. Rejecting the assumption that Scandinavia is a group of passive states that are without influence, my analysis explains how and why a small group of like-minded societies work collectively through international institutions and as norm entrepreneurs to advance particular visions of the global good society. Scandinavia, in important and subtle ways, has an influence on how the international system evolves.

101

This book connects to a broader literature that explores the role of small states in international relations.[2] Transnational studies of international agenda setting typically focus on international organizations and/or social movements (e.g., the works of Thomas Risse, Kathryn Sikkink, Michael Barnett, Martha Finnemore, Nancy Naples, and Manisha Desai). The roles of individuals who serve as catalysts for political change and bring with them the experience of living in a distinct polity with unique policy legacies are an important aspect of global governance. With the exception of Sidney Tarrow's work on transnational activists or "rooted cosmopolitans," the role of individuals is an often-neglected dimension of world politics.

Is the capacity to influence the international system and contribute to the direction and substance of European integration limited to the five northern European countries that have been our focus? Certainly not. However, it is notable that all eyes turn to Oslo when the Nobel Peace Prize is awarded annually. Despite like-minded agendas, other governments and societies have yet to cultivate the global niche associated with Scandinavianism. Even though Canada is often considered a norm entrepreneur, advocating agendas similar to Norway and implementing policies praised by Scandinavian leaders, Canadians are in the shadow of U.S. power and dependence and face challenges of governance and resource management at home. And the Benelux area (Belgium, the Netherlands, and Luxembourg), while well positioned to influence the EU in important directions, is a partner, as opposed to a leader, in international institutions. Dutch contributions to international aid policy are consistent with Scandinavian norms, yet in other areas, the Dutch are less likely to be setting the global agenda.[3] Instead, these like-minded governments and societies are coalition partners, working with Scandinavians to advocate for global change in the world system.

At the height of U.S. hegemony, international relations scholar Robert Keohane examined how the weak can influence the strong. In "The Big Influence of Small Allies" (*Foreign Policy*, 1971), Keohane demonstrated how multilateral and bilateral arrangements permit smaller powers to exert their authority over larger, more powerful states such as the United States: "like an elephant yoked to a team of lesser animals, the United States is linked to smaller and weaker allies . . . these are the badgers, mice and pigeons—if not the doves—of international politics, and in many cases they have been able to lead the elephant."[4] The quiet role of coalitions of like-minded states, with consistent agendas and prominent advocates, is one of the least understood aspects of how power is exercised in international relations.

Scandinavia, as this book has shown, not only seeks to influence the United States but also asserts its ideals in shaping the future direction of European-wide cooperation as well as the agendas of major international institutions. Scandinavia and Scandinavians exercise their influence through international activism predicated on a collective vision of the global good society and legitimated by a lengthy period of experimentation at home. Even the smallest of these states (Iceland) has elevated attention to the rights of small states through international activism.

As argued here, Scandinavia is an appropriate site for norm entrepreneurship. The issues and problems of transnational interconnectedness have evolved in new and important directions. Structural changes in international politics have positioned Scandinavia to play an important role on the international stage. No longer divided between East and West, Scandinavians are, now more than ever, redefining how others view security. New threats—from global terrorist networks to transnational environmental disasters—require collective action by governments and creative new solutions. Cold War great power doctrine is a poor fit with the redefinition of threats to security and stability. The international political economy has evolved from a system where economic prosperity depended on the export of industrial goods to one with an enhanced reliance on services and technology sectors. Throughout the world, governments increasingly collaborate with one another to compete in the global economy—pooling their sovereignty in unprecedented ways. How is Scandinavia seeking to set the agenda in the world today?

International transformations require new thinking, and prominent Scandinavians are leading the way. Members of these societies place greater trust in governance than is typical of more neoliberal societies, and Scandinavian foreign-policy makers view international collaboration and multilateralism as progress. Scandinavian activism takes multiple forms—from individual initiatives to bilateral and multilateral efforts to create new institutions or revitalize existing partnerships (such as Swedish and Finnish agenda setting and Danish heel dragging in the EU).

New ideas concerning conflict management, poverty avoidance, the role of science and technology, measures to improve the environment, and global governance are examples of Scandinavia's role in world politics today. Not all Scandinavian initiatives are novel: there are instances when Scandinavia is as much a follower as a leader. However, in the international community of states, the world would be different without Scandinavian norm entrepreneurship.

The following discussion elaborates on how Scandinavia is redefining its presence in world politics.

RETHINKING SECURITY

Scandinavia has expanded the international agenda in security policy making. By raising awareness of new risks (from Chernobyl and other transnational environmental threats to global trafficking in women), local experience is translated into issues on the agendas of larger, more powerful states and in a variety of forums (the UN, the Nordic Council, the EU, the OSCE, and NATO).

Scandinavia is also redefining how small states contribute to global security. For example, Swedish and Finnish defense planners initiated new security measures in the Amsterdam Treaty, as part of the EU's Common Foreign and Security Policy. The framework to create a common European defense structure will be different with Europe's northernmost partners at the table because these governments have experimented with alternative means of conflict prevention, combining strategies of reassurance and deterrence.

In a major reversal of previous security policy-making practices, the Swedes are pursuing a much more active role. In his visit to the United States in the spring of 2002, Sweden's defense minister Bjorn von Sydow met with U.S. deputy defense secretary Paul Wolfowitz to discuss the situation in Afghanistan and the Balkans. The Swedish government has volunteered to provide assistance from its engineering corps to rebuild Kabul and favors a greater role for Swedish (and other Nordic) troops in the Balkans.[5]

In recent decades, Scandinavian aid organizations and government ministries have reassessed how they provide assistance to the developed world. Informed by the New International Economic Order debates of the 1970s and increasingly concerned about throwing resources at a problem without providing long-term solutions, Scandinavians have evolved new mechanisms of assistance.

Scandinavians have been described as rational humanitarians who embrace progress and harness a better society through the use of state authority. The disillusionment with past efforts to create a better world (from housing policy to other experiments with centralized planning) have not deterred Scandinavians from embracing scientific and technological discoveries designed to improve or enhance the collective good.

In the transition to an Internet age, Scandinavians have emerged as world leaders. Anticipating the potential of the new technology, government leaders adopted policies to enable a rapid dispersal of computers and technological know-how within these societies. In Scandinavia, favorable terms for purchasing computers and incentives to convert the population to a high level of "IT-literacy" as part of national commitments to higher education have led these countries to rank above other European states in the new "e-economy."[6] Prominent firms—Nokia of Finland and Ericsson of Sweden—lead the development of new technologies—particularly in mobile phones and infrastructure. A new class of entrepreneurs has emerged in the Nordic countries who are global players in the industry. The reputation of Scandinavians as "e-vikings" has led international firms such as Microsoft, Oracle, and Intel to locate subsidiaries in Scandinavia. National policies (such as high levels of investment in research and development) have encouraged a rapid integration of technological competence in these countries.

As societies seek to stem the effects of pollution on the environment, Scandinavians provide global leadership. Gro Harlem Brundtland's UN Commission on the Environment (1987) advocated the inclusion of ecological criteria in economic development and redefined how governments, NGOs, and states engage these questions. Relying on national legacies of conservationism and "sustainable development," Scandinavia also exports products designed to improve the environment. The new airport in China, for example, featured a Swedish system of vehicle-free ramps, designed to reduce the number of vehicles required to service airplanes and significantly lessen carbon emissions.[7] Engineers in northern Europe are systematically integrating sustainable technologies into global products, designed to change the way the world lives and works.

Under Gro Harlem Brundtland's leadership, the World Health Organization (WHO) launched a controversial international campaign to ban tobacco advertising.[8] Designed to improve global health, this initiative has serious implications for U.S. companies—the largest producers of tobacco products in the world. The International Tobacco Control Regime restrictions have been taken seriously in Norway, where a ban against smoking is in effect. In other European states, the appropriateness of access to tobacco products has become an item on the political agenda (for example, in France). This is an issue/area where the United States has *not* emerged as a norm leader but where Scandinavians have again led the way.

Another initiative attracting international attention is the Norwegian government's anti-bullying policy in the school system. The world's foremost expert on bullying is an academic at the University of Bergen in Norway. And the government, under the leadership of Prime Minister Kjell Magne Bondevik, has established an international standard in recognizing the need to protect children from aggression by other children.

For Norwegian norm entrepreneurs, a significant threat to international peace and security is the availability of small arms. The UN Programme of Action on Small Arms and Light Weapons is supported financially by the Norwegian government and is bringing together governments to develop plans to regulate weapons transfers.[9] And as the international community coped with the devastating consequences of the 2004 tsunami in Indonesia, Sri Lanka, Thailand, and India, the UN undersecretary-general for humanitarian affairs and emergency relief coordinator Jan Egeland criticized the Bush administration for failing to provide adequate humanitarian and disaster aid immediately following the crisis. As the situation evolved, the United States and other countries, along with private donors, contributed more generously, leading Egeland to later commend their efforts.

At the Stockholm International Forum in April 2002, Swedish prime minister Goran Persson called on states to join those who have ratified the Rome Statute, the treaty creating a permanent international criminal court. Throughout Scandinavia, new initiatives to strengthen international cooperation and codify appropriate standards of behavior or norms are being formulated or actions are being taken to refine those in existence.

Diversity is the issue that threatens to undermine Scandinavia's identity and it could ultimately jeopardize the legitimacy of Scandinavian leadership abroad. Even as political leaders vigorously debate how diversity should be managed, the image of the new Scandinavia is evolving. Contemporary Scandinavian films, including the Swedish film *Wings of Glass*, and crime fiction writers portray ethnically divided societies, while government commissions advocate equal treatment for all citizens. However, international incidents of hate crimes against immigrants have attracted worldwide media attention. These high-profile cases raise questions in and out of Scandinavia, as these societies are confronting ever-increasing diversity at home. According to Keya Izol, head of the Federation of Kurdish Associations in Sweden, "there are places just outside of Stockholm where the entire population is foreign. These people aren't living in Sweden at all."[10] In Denmark and Norway, the growing popularity of political parties seeking to tighten border controls and limit immigration has been viewed critically by observers as evidence that these societies are not as tolerant and freedom-loving as they proclaim. Unless this challenge is reconciled, Scandinavia will lose its moral authority as the conscience of the international community.

CONCLUSION

Although norm entrepreneurship is not limited to this distinct corner of Europe, Scandinavia and Scandinavians are more likely than others to be found pursuing efforts to change the way the international system functions. The origins of this role can be traced to four defining features of Scandinavian societies: rural values, religion in society, economic dependence on natural resources, and the role of law in society. These have shaped the worldviews of generations of individual leaders who contribute to agenda setting within and outside the state.

Prominent Scandinavians are transnational actors, strengthening global norms in particular issues/areas. By awarding the most prestigious international prize in the world, the Nobel Peace Prize, Norwegians can help set the global agenda and place themselves in the international spotlight as doves in world politics. Norway has found a niche in world politics, distinct from its neighbors Sweden, Denmark, and Finland, who are embedded in the EU's agenda-setting process.

An old Icelandic poem reads, "People die, your livestock dies; the one thing that does not die is your reputation."[11] As Jonathan Mercer argues, reputations are important to states.[12] Other, more powerful states may not have the capacity to lead in particular issues/areas—ceding authority to small states, or other configurations of authority, such as the EU. According to human rights leaders, Scandinavia's reputation for longstanding commitments to social justice is well established. "None of us in the human rights community would think of appealing to the U.S. for support for upholding a human rights case—maybe to Canada, to Norway or to Sweden—but not to the U.S."[13]

Scandinavia's reputation abroad depends on its capacity to continue to articulate a common vision without being splintered by challenges at home. Scandinavia is increasingly subject to international scrutiny, which helps redefine its own understanding of self. With changes in global society—growing conflict within and between states, ethnic tensions, human rights abuses, and aggravated conditions for those seeking prosperity—Scandinavia is, now more than ever, well positioned to play a global role.

There are four important lessons to be drawn from this book. First, Scandinavia and Scandinavians have played a role in the international system that predates globalization and the establishment of the social democratic welfare state. Second, prominent leaders from these societies are transnational actors, advocating shared values abroad—in multilateral, bilateral, and unilateral initiatives—and through awarding the Nobel Peace Prize. In the words of 2004 Nobel Peace Prize winner Wangari Maathai, an environmental activist from Kenya,

> I believe the Nobel Committee recognized the links between the environment, democracy and peace and sought to bring them to worldwide attention with the Peace Prize that I am accepting. . . . The committee, I believe, is seeking to encourage community efforts to restore the earth at a time when we face the ecological crises of deforestation, desertification, water scarcity and a lack of biological diversity. Unless we properly manage resources like forests, water, land, minerals and oil, we will not win the fight against poverty.[14]

Third, the only threat to Scandinavia's capacity to play a leading role is the challenges of adhering to its own global standards—particularly, as I argue here, in the transition to multicultural societies. Fourth and finally, a note of caution: beware of delegations from northern Europe—they have an agenda, and they are as determined and tenacious as earlier warriors emanating from this corner of the globe.

NOTES

1. Gylfi Gislason, "In Defense of Small Nations," in "The Nordic Enigma," *Daedalus* 113 (Winter 1984): 210.

2. See Christine Ingebritsen, Iver Neumann, Sieglinde Gstohl, and Jessica Beyer (eds.), *Small States in International Relations* (Reykjavik and Seattle: University of Iceland and University of Washington Press, 2004).

3. Paulette Kurzer has documented Dutch exceptionalism within the EU (national drug policy).

4. Robert Keohane, "The Big Influence of Small Allies," *Foreign Policy*, no. 2 (1971): 161.

5. Nora Boustany, "Military Missions in Mind as Swedish Minister Visits," *The Washington Post*, May 29, 2002.

6. See Christopher Brown-Humes, "E-Vikings Blaze the Online Trail," *Nordic Information* (May 11, 2000).

7. Marcus Gibson, "Green Scene: Latest Products to Protect the Environment," *Scandinavian Review* 86, no. 3 (Winter 1998/99): 17.

8. With thanks to Paulette Kurzer, professor of political science, University of Arizona, whose research examines moral dimensions in European politics and society.

9. "Putting Guns in Their Place: A New Publication by the Centre for Humanitarian Dialogue," www.hdcentre.org/?aid=121. Accessed November 28, 2005.

10. Carol Williams, "Price of Freedom: In Blood," *The Los Angeles Times*, March 7, 2002, p. A6.

11. Robert Kunzig, "Blood of the Vikings," *Discover* 19 (December 1998): 99.

12. Jonathan Mercer, *Reputation and International Politics* (Ithaca, NY: Cornell University Press, 1996).

13. Mrs. Coomaraswamy, Sri Lankan human rights activist, cited in Thomas Friedman, "Bush's Shame," *New York Times*, August 4, 2002.

14. Wangari Maathai, 2004 Nobel Peace Prize recipient, in the *New York Times*, December 10, 2004, p. A31.

Bibliography

Aaberg, Ingrid. "Kvinnor paa troskeln till ny tid." *Kyrkohistorisk Aarskrift* 94 (1994): 77–78.

Abrams, Irwin. "Heroines of Peace." www.nobel.se/peace/articles/heroines/index .html. Accessed November 28, 2005.

Ahtisaari, Martti. "Future of the Balkans." *Presidents and Prime Ministers* 9, no. 1 (2000): 22.

Alho, Olli, ed. *Finland: A Cultural Encyclopedia.* Helsinki: Finnish Literature Society, 1997.

Andenaes, Mads T., and Ingeborg Wilberg. *The Constitution of Norway.* Oslo: Universitetsforlaget, 1987.

Andersen, Jorgen Goul, and Jens Hoff. *Democracy and Citizenship in Scandinavia.* New York: Palgrave, 2001.

Arnason, Ragnar. *The Icelandic Fisheries.* Oxford, UK: Fishing News Books, 1995.

Arter, David. "Small State Influence within the EU: The Case of Finland's 'Northern Dimension Initiative.'" *Journal of Common Market Studies* 38 (2000): 677–697.

Barnes, Hilary. "Nordic Togetherness: Let Us Count the Ways." *Scandinavian Review* 86, no. 2 (1998): 68–75.

Barros, James. *Trygve Lie and the Cold War: The UN Secretary-General Pursues Peace 1946–1953.* DeKalb: Northern Illinois University Press, 1989.

Barthe, Magne, and Else Marie Brodshaug. *Nordisk sikkerhet—paa vei mot EU og NATO.* Oslo: Institut for Fedsforskning, 1997.

Bensinger, Ari. "The Call on Nokia: Buy." *Business Week Online,* January 7, 2003.

Bering, Henrik. "Denmark, the Euro, and the Fear of the Foreign." *Policy Review,* no. 104 (2000): 63–73.

Bildt, Carl. "The Baltic Litmus Test." *Foreign Affairs* 73, no. 5 (1994): 72–86.

Bjorklund, Oddvar. *Marcus Thrane: Sosialistleder I et u-land.* Oslo: Tiden Norsk Forlag, 1970.

Boustany, Nora. "Military Missions in Mind as Swedish Minister Visits." *The Washington Post,* May 29, 2002.

Brekke, N. G. *Kultur Historisk Vegbok*. Bergen, Norway: Vestkyst, 1993.

Brown-Humes, Christopher. "E-Vikings Blaze the Online Trail." *Nordic Information*, May 11, 2000.

Bruni, Frank. "A Nation that Exports Oil, Herring and Peace." *New York Times*, December 21, 2002.

Burgess, Philip. *Elite Images and Foreign Policy Outcomes*. Columbus: Ohio State University Press, 1968.

Byock, Jesse. *Viking Age Iceland*. London: Penguin Books, 2001.

Caporaso, James. "Across the Great Divide: Integrating Comparative and International Politics." *International Studies Quarterly* 41 (1997): 563–592.

Cavendish, Richard. "The Birth of Urho Kekkonen." *History Today* 50, no. 9 (2000): 54.

Centre for Humanitarian Dialogue. "Putting Guns in Their Place: A New Publication by the Centre for Humanitarian Dialogue." www.hdcentre.org/?aid=121. Accessed November 28, 2005.

Chemical and Engineering News. "Iceland Plans Carbon-Free Economy." Vol. 79, no. 33 (2001): 31.

Childs, Marquis. *The Middle Way*. New Haven, CT: Yale University Press, 1936.

Clark, Ann Marie. *Diplomacy of Conscience: Amnesty International and Changing Human Rights Norms*. Princeton, NJ: Princeton University Press, 2001.

Cohat, Yves. *The Vikings: Lords of the Seas*. New York: Harry N. Abrams Inc., 1992.

Coleman, David, and Eskil Wadensjo. *Immigration to Denmark: International and National Perspectives*. Aarhus, Denmark: Aarhus University Press, 1999.

Cotrell, John. *Scandinavia*. Amsterdam: Time-Life Books, 1985.

Crystal, David. *The Cambridge Biographical Encyclopedia*. Cambridge, UK: Cambridge University Press, 1994.

Daedalus. "The Nordic Enigma." Entire issue. Vol. 113, no. 1 (Winter 1984).

Danish Ministry of Foreign Affairs. "One Europe: Programme of the Danish Presidency of the EU, Second Half of 2002." Copenhagen: Royal Danish Ministry of Foreign Affairs, 2002.

Davies, Norman. *Europe: A History*. Oxford, UK: Oxford University Press, 1996.

Davis, Morris. *Iceland Extends Its Fisheries Limits: A Political Analysis*. Oslo: Universitetsforlaget, 1963.

Derry, T. K. *A History of Scandinavia*. Minneapolis: University of Minnesota Press, 1979.

Dugger, Celia. "After Ferocious Fighting, Sri Lanka Struggles with Peace." *New York Times*, April 9, 2002.

Economist, The. "Jens Stoltenberg: Cautious PM." July 22, 2000.

Economist, The. "Odd Man Out under Oddson." March 14, 1992.

Economist, The. "Survey of the Nordic Countries." June 14, 2003.

Egeland, Jan. *Impotent Superpower—Potent Small State*. Oslo: Norwegian University Press, 1988.

Einhorn, Eric, and John Logue. *Modern Welfare States: Scandinavian Politics and Policy in the Global Age*. Westport, CT: Praeger, 2003.

Elliston, Herbert B. *Finland Fights*. Boston: Little, Brown and Company, 1940.

Engellau, Patrick, and Ulf Henning. *Nordic Views and Values*. Stockholm: The Nordic Council, 1984.

Enoch, Yael. "The Intolerance of a Tolerant People: Ethnic Relations in Denmark." *Ethnic and Racial Studies* 17, no. 2 (1994): 282–300.

Environmental Science and Technology. "Danes Get the Lead Out." Vol. 35, no. 3 (2001): 63A.

Eriksen, Thomas Hylland. "Globalization and Norwegian Identity." *Nytt fra Norge*. Oslo: Norwegian Ministry of Foreign Affairs, 1996.

Esaiasson, Peter, and Knut Heidar, eds. *Beyond Westminster and Congress: The Nordic Experience*. Columbus: Ohio State University Press, 2000.

Esping-Andersen, Gøsta. *Politics against Markets*. Princeton, NJ: Princeton University Press, 1985.

European Union Commission. "EU Criticizes Russia's Force in Chechnya." *Europe*, no. 392 (2000): S-3.

European Union Commission. "The Implementation of a Northern Dimension for the Policies of the European Union." Conclusions adopted by the European Council of Ministers on 31 May 1999. http://europa.ceu.int/comm/external_relations/north_dim/doc/pres_concl_06_99.htm. Accessed November 28, 2005.

European Union Commission. "A Northern Dimension for the Policies of the Union." Communication from the Commission. COM (1998) 589 final (November 25, 1998). http://europa.eu.int/comm/external_relations/north_dim/doc/com1998_0589en.pdf. Accessed November 28, 2005.

Financial Times. "Scandinavia Tops World League Table on the Environment." February 2–3, 2002.

Finnish Institute of Migration. www.migrationinstitute.fi/db/articles/art.php?artid=34. Accessed November 28, 2005.

Finnish Ministry of Foreign Affairs. "The Economic Significance of EU Membership for Finland." http://virtual.finland.fi.

Finnish Ministry of Foreign Affairs. *Human Rights and Finland's Foreign Policy*. Helsinki: Edita, 2001.

Friedman, Thomas. "Bush's Shame." *New York Times*, August 4, 2002.

Geremek, Bronislaw. "Current Challenges for the OSCE and the Role of the Chairmanship." *Security Policy Library*, no. 10. Oslo: The Norwegian Atlantic Committee, 1998.

Gibbs, David. "Dag Hammarskjold, the United Nations and the Congo Crisis of 1960–61: A Reinterpretation." *The Journal of Modern African Studies* 31, no. 1 (1993): 163–74.

Gibson, Marcus. "Green Scene: Latest Products to Protect the Environment." *Scandinavian Review* 86, no. 3 (1998/99): 17–26.

Gislason, Gylfi. "In Defense of Small Nations." In "The Nordic Enigma." *Daedalus* 113 (Winter 1984).

Goetschel, Laurent. "The Foreign and Security Interests of Small States in Today's Europe." *Small States Inside and Outside the European Union: Interests and Policies*. Boston: Kluwer Academic Publishers, 1998.

Gradin, Anita. "Sweden's Role in the EU." Presentation at the University of Washington, Seattle, Spring 2001.

Gulicova-Grethe, Maria. "Intpol—Denmark: The Politics of Adaptation and Integration in Denmark." Manuscript, 1993.

Gupte, Pranay, and Rahul Singh. "Money! Guns! Corruption!" *Forbes* (July 1997): 112.

Guttmann, Robert. "Danish Business Goes Global." *Europe* 339 (1994): 10–12.

Hadenius, Stig. *The Riksdag in Focus: Swedish History in a Parliamentary Perspective.* Stockholm: Berlings Arlov, 1997.

Hall, Peter. *The Political Power of Economic Ideas.* Princeton, NJ: Princeton University Press, 1989.

Hansen, Lene, and Ole Wæver, eds. *European Integration and National Identity: The Challenge of the Nordic States.* London: Routledge, 2002.

Hart, Jeffrey. *The Anglo-Icelandic Cod War of 1972–1973: A Case Study of a Fishery Dispute.* Berkeley: Institute of International Studies, University of California, 1976.

Haslam, Gerald Myron. *Clash of Cultures.* New York: Peter Lang Publishers, 1984.

Heidar, Knut. *Norway: Elites on Trial.* Boulder, CO: Westview Press, 2001.

Helle, Knut, ed. *The Cambridge History of Scandinavia: Volume I Prehistory to 1520.* Cambridge, UK: Cambridge University Press, 2003.

Helsingin Sanomat. "Government Calls for More Immigrants." 2004. www .helsinginsanomat.fi/English/article/1076154576658. Accessed November 28, 2005.

Hermele, Kenneth. "A Letter from Sweden: The Bishops Take the Lead." *Monthly Review* 45, no. 9 (1994): 30–33.

Hernes, Gudmund. *Makt og Styring.* Oslo: Gyldendal Norsk Forlag, 1983.

Holst, Johan Jorgen, ed. *Norwegian Foreign Policy in the 1980s.* Oslo: Norwegian University Press, 1985.

Holst, Johan Jørgen. "Reflections on the Making of a Tenuous Peace, or the Transformation of Images of the Middle East Conflict." Lecture presented at the School of International and Public Affairs, Columbia University, New York, September 28, 1993.

Hugus, Frank. "Hans Christian Andersen: The Storyteller as Social Critic." *Scandinavian Review* 87 (1999): 29–36.

Huntford, Roland. *Nansen: The Explorer as Hero.* London: Gerald Duckworth and Company, 1997.

Hurrell, Andrew. "International Society and the Study of Regimes: A Reflective Approach." *Regime Theory and International Relations,* ed. Volker Rittenberger. Oxford, UK: Clarendon Press, 1993.

Iceland Ministry for Foreign Affairs. *British Aggression in Icelandic Waters.* Reykjavik, 1959.

Ingebritsen, Christine. *The Nordic States and European Unity.* Ithaca, NY: Cornell University Press, 1998.

Ingebritsen, Christine. "Norm Entrepreneurs: Scandinavia's Role in World Politics." *Cooperation and Conflict* 37 (2002): 11–23.

Ingebritsen, Christine, Iver Neumann, Sieglinde Gstohl, and Jessica Beyer, eds. *Small States in International Relations.* Reykjavik and Seattle: University of Iceland and University of Washington Press, 2006.

Jagland, Thorbjorn. "On Norway and the European Defence Policy." Speech to the Storting, June 9, 2000. Oslo: Norwegian Foreign Ministry.

Johnsson, Gerd. *Gender Equality between Women and Men in Development Cooperation.* Stockholm: Swedish Ministry of Foreign Affairs, 1998.

Jones, Dorothy. "The Example of Dag Hammarskjold." *The Christian Century* 111, no. 32 (1994): 1047–1051.

Jones, S. Shepard. *The Scandinavian States and the League of Nations.* Princeton, NJ: Princeton University Press and New York: American Scandinavian Foundation, 1939.

Katzenstein, Peter J. *Small States in World Markets.* Ithaca, NY: Cornell University Press, 1985.

Keohane, Robert. "The Big Influence of Small Allies." *Foreign Policy*, no. 2 (1971): 161–182.

Keough, Jessie. "Visions of Europe: Small States and European Policies: The Influence of Finland and Sweden upon the European Union's Agenda." Paper presented at the University of Washington, June 12, 2001.

Kiel, Anne Cohen. *Continuity and Change.* Oslo: Scandinavian University Press, 1993.

Klotz, Audie. *Norms in International Relations.* Ithaca, NY: Cornell University Press, 1995.

Knudsen, Tim, ed. *Den nordiske protestantisme og velfaerdsstaten.* Aarhus, Denmark: Universitetsforlag, 2000.

Koivukangas, Olavi. "Foreigners in Finland." *Politics and Society*, Virtual Finland. http://virtual.finland.ni/netcomm/news/showarticle.asp?intNWSAID=25787. Accessed November 28, 2005.

Kronsell, Annica. "Can Small States Influence EU Norms? Insights from Sweden's Participation in the Field of Environmental Politics." Working paper presented at the conference "The EU and Scandinavia Today," The EU Center of Seattle, University of Washington, February 1–2, 2001.

Kunzig, Robert. "Blood of the Vikings." *Discover* 19 (1998): 90–100.

Kurlansky, Mark. *Cod: A Biography of the Fish that Changed the World.* New York: Walker and Company, 1997.

Kurzer, Paulette. *Business and Banking: Political Change and Economic Integration in Western Europe.* Ithaca, NY: Cornell University Press, 1993.

Kurzer, Paulette. *Markets and Moral Regulation: Cultural Change in the European Union.* Cambridge, UK: Cambridge University Press, 2001.

LaBarba, Liane. "Nokia Promises Growth Despite Down Market." *Telephony* (2002).

Langdon-Davies, John. *Invasion in the Snow.* Boston: Houghton Mifflin Company, 1941.

Larsen, Karen. *A History of Norway.* Princeton, NJ: Princeton University Press, 1950.

Lauring, Palle. *A History of Denmark.* Copenhagen: Host and Sons Forlag, 1960.

Lavery, Jason. "Remembering Kekkonen." *Scandinavian Review* 88, no. 3 (2001): 5–13.

Lawler, Peter. "Scandinavian Exceptionalism and European Union." *The Journal of Common Market Studies* 34, no. 4 (1997): 565–594.

Lehtonen, Tuomas. *Europe's Northern Frontier: Perspectives on Finland's Western Identity.* Porvoo, Finland: Finnish National Fund for Research and Development, 1999.

Leiren, Terje. *Marcus Thrane: A Norwegian Radical in America.* Northfield, MN: Norwegian American Historical Association, 1987.

Libæk, Ivar, and Øyvind Stenersen. *A History of Norway: From the Ice Age to the Age of Petroleum.* Oslo: Grøndahl Dreyer, 1999.

Lieberfeld, Daniel. "Small Is Credible: Norway's Niche in International Dispute Settlement." *Negotiation Journal* 11, no. 3 (1995): 201–207.

Linder, Doris. "Equality for Women: The Contribution of Scandinavian Women at the United Nations, 1946–66." *Scandinavian Studies* 73, no. 2 (2001): 165–209.

Lindh, Anna. "Create a Worldwide Culture of Conflict Prevention." *International Herald Tribune*, September 18, 1999, p. 6.

Lower, Eldborg. "Defence Policy Challenges for the Year 2000." Oslo: Norwegian Ministry of Defence, January 18, 2001, http://odin.dep.no.

Ludlow, Peter. "Scandinavia between the Great Powers: Attempts at Mediation in the First Year of the Second World War." *Historisk Tidskrift* 1 (1974): 1–58.

McMorrow, Marilyn. Speech presented at the Holst Symposium on Norwegian Foreign Policy Making, University of Washington, Seattle, October 11, 2001.

McNeil, Donald. "An Icelandic Battle of Wildlife Versus Voltage." *New York Times.* www.nytimes.com, July 16, 2002.

Mercer, Jonathan. *Reputation and International Politics.* Ithaca, NY: Cornell University Press, 1996.

Mintner, William. "The Impossible Neutrality: Sweden's Role under Olof Palme." *Africa Today* 43, no. 1 (1996): 95–98.

Misgeld, Klaus, Karl Molin, and Klas Amark. *Creating Social Democracy.* University Park: Pennsylvania State University Press, 1992.

Moberg, V. "Life in the Villages." *Nordic Views and Values*, ed. Patrick Engellau and Ulf Henning. Stockholm: The Nordic Council, 1984.

Molin, Lennart. "Not for Ourselves Alone." *The Ecumenical Review* 52 (2000): 172–180.

Moravscik, Andrew. *The Choice for Europe: Social Purpose and State Power from Messina to Maastricht.* Ithaca, NY: Cornell University Press, 1998.

Mouritzen, Hans. "The Nordic Model as a Foreign Policy Instrument: Its Rise and Fall." *Journal of Peace Research* 32, no. 1 (1995): 9–21.

Nannestad, Peter. *Solidaritetens Pris: Holdningen til invandrere og flygtninge I Danmark 1987–1993.* Aarhus, Denmark: Aarhus Universitetsforlag, 1999.

Naples, Nancy, and Manisha Desai, eds. *Women's Activism and Globalization: Linking Local Struggles and Transnational Politics.* London: Routledge, 2002.

NATO Nytt. Den Norske Atlanterhavscomite. NATO Public Diplomacy Division. Brussels: NATO, 2001.

Neumann, Iver. *Norge—en kritikk: begrepsmakt I Europa-debatten.* Oslo: Pax, 2001.

Neumann, Iver. *Russia and the Idea of Europe: Identity and International Relations.* London: Routledge, 1996.

News of Norway. "Modern Norway: Human Rights." Vol. 57, no. 1 (2000): 6–7.

News of Norway. "Norway Pledges Economic Support for Middle East Peace." Vol. 50, no. 7 (October 1993): 1.

Nordal, Johannes, and Valdimar Kristinsson. *Iceland: 874–1974*. Reykjavik: The Central Bank of Iceland, 1975.

Nordic Council. *The Source of Liberty: The Nordic Contribution to Europe*. Stockholm: Nordic Council, 1992.

Nordic Council of Ministers. "Baltic Projects Get Go-Ahead." *Norden: The Top of Europe*, no. 3 (1991).

Norwegian Government. "News from Norway," April 20, 2001.

Norwegian Ministry of Foreign Affairs, "Focus on Norwegian Development Cooperation" (Report to Parliament). Oslo: Norwegian Ministry of Foreign Affairs, 2002. www.dep.no/filarkiv/156542/Utredning-nr-13-Engelsk.pdf. Accessed November 29, 2005.

Norwegian Ministry of Foreign Affairs. "Human Rights 1999: Annual Report on Norwegian Efforts to Promote Human Rights." Oslo, Norwegian Ministry of Foreign Affairs, 1999. www.dep.no/filarkiv/132960/mreng.pdf. Accessed November 29, 2005.

Norwegian Ministry of Foreign Affairs. "Norwegian Minke Whaling." odin.dep .no/odin/engelsk/norway/environment/o32001-990108/. Accessed November 29, 2005.

Olafsson, Bjorn. *Small States in the Global System*. Aldershot, UK: Ashgate Publishers, 1998.

Olweus, Dan. *Bullying at School: What We Know and What We Can Do*. Oxford, UK: Blackwell, 1993.

Palsson, Gisli, and E. Paul Durrenberger. *Images of Contemporary Iceland*. Iowa City: University of Iowa Press, 1996.

Pentilla, Risto. *Finland's Search for Security through Defense, 1944–89*. London: Macmillan, 1991.

Petersson, Olof. *The Government and Politics of the Nordic Countries*. Stockholm: Fritzes, 1994.

Pipes, Daniel, and Lars Hedegaard. "Something Rotten in Denmark?" *Jerusalem Post*, August 28, 2002.

Pontusson, Jonas. "At the End of the Third Road: Swedish Social Democracy in Crisis." *Politics and Society* 20, no. 3 (September 1992): 305–332.

Pontusson, Jonas. *The Limits of Social Democracy: Investment Politics in Sweden*. Ithaca, NY: Cornell University Press, 1992.

Pred, Allan. *Even in Sweden: Racisms, Racialized Spaces and the Popular Geographical Imagination*. Berkeley: University of California Press, 2000.

Reus-Smit, Chris. *The Moral Purpose of the State*. Princeton, NJ: Princeton University Press, 1999.

Ries, Tomas. *Cold Will: The Defence of Finland*. London: Brassey's Defence Publishers, 1988.

Rigby, Andrew. "Unofficial Nonviolent Intervention: Examples from the Israeli-Palestinian Conflict." *Journal of Peace Research* 32, no. 4 (1995): 453–467.

Riis, Ole. "The Role of Religion in Legitimating the Modern Structuration of Society." *Acta Sociologica* 32, no. 2 (June 1989): 137–154.

Ringmar, Erik. "Re-Imagining Sweden: The Rhetorical Debate over EU Membership." *Scandinavian Journal of History* 23, nos. 1–2 (1998): 45–63.

Rittberger, Volker, ed. *Regime Theory and International Relations*. Oxford: Clarendon Press, 1993.

Rombel, Adam. "Island Nation Rides the Tech Tides." *Global Finance* 16, no. 10 (2002): 88–90.

Rothstein, Bo. *Just Institutions Matter: The Moral and Political Logic of the Welfare State*. Cambridge, UK: Cambridge University Press, 1998.

Sains, Ariane. "Sweden Takes the EU Helm." *Europe*, no. 402 (December/January 2000–2001): 6–8.

Sandemose, Aksel. *A Fugitive Crosses His Tracks*. New York: Knopf, 1936.

Satterfield, David, James Zogby, and Ian Lustick. "Symposium: Reexamining the Arab-Israeli Peace Process." *Middle East Policy* 4, nos. 1–2 (1995): 72–87.

"Scandinavia in Europe." Conference Proceedings, University of Washington, Seattle, February 1–2, 2001.

Scott, Franklin D. *Sweden: The Nation's History*. Carbondale: Southern Illinois University Press, 1988.

Senghaas, Dieter. *The European Experience: A Historical Critique of Development Theory*. UK: Berg, 1982.

Shlaim, Avi. "The Oslo Accord." *The Journal of Palestine Studies* 23, no. 3 (Spring 1994): 24–40.

Sigvaldsson, Herluf. "The International Whaling Commission: The Transition from a 'Whaling Club' to a 'Preservationist Club.'" *Cooperation and Conflict* 31, no. 3 (1996): 311–352.

Sorensen, Oystein. *Fridtjof Nansen: Mannen og myten*. Oslo: Universitetsforlaget, 1993.

Sorensen, Torkil. "Rent Miljo—en nordisk maerkesag." *Politik I Norden*, no. 2 (March/April 2001): 11–14.

Stang, Fredrik. "The Nobel Prize for 1922." Speech by the chairman of the Nobel Committee, Oslo, 1922. www.Nobel.se/peace/laureates/1922/press.html. Accessed November 29, 2005.

Steinmo, Sven. "Globalization and Taxation: Challenges to the Swedish Welfare State." *Comparative Political Studies* 35, no. 7 (September 2002): 839–862.

Stoltenberg, Thorvald. "Love of Man Is Practical Policy." *The Fridtjof Nansen Memorial Lectures*. Oslo: The Norwegian Academy of Science and Letters and the Norwegian Foreign Ministry, 1990.

Stoltenberg, Thorvald. "Norway, Peace Negotiations, Human Rights: Effects and Influences." Holst Symposium on Norwegian Foreign Policy, University of Washington, Seattle, October 24, 1996.

Svåsand, Lars. "The Early Organization Society in Norway." *Scandinavian Journal of History* 5, no. 3 (1980): 185–196.

Svensk Turistforeningens Forlag. *Arets Bilder*. Stockholm: Svenska Turistforeningens Forlag, 1955.

Swedish Immigration Board. *Sweden: A General Introduction for Immigrants*. Varnamo, Sweden: AB Falths Tryckeri, 1989.

Swedish Ministry of Foreign Affairs. "Preventing Violent Conflict—A Swedish Action Plan." *UD Info* (May 1999): 1–51.

Swedish Ministry of Industry, Employment and Communications. *Working towards Sustainable Development*. Stockholm: Swedish Ministry of Industry , 2001.

Tarrow, Sidney. The New Transnational Activism. Book manuscript, forthcoming.

Taylor, William, and Paul Cole. *Nordic Defense: Comparative Decision Making*. Lexington, KY: DC Heath and Company, 1985.

Thorhallsson, Baldur. *The Role of Small States in the European Union*. Aldershot, UK: Ashgate Press, 2000.

Tiersky, Ronald. *Euro-Skepticism: A Reader*. Lanham, MD: Rowman and Littlefield Publishers, 2001.

Time International. "Visionaries." December 10, 1998.

Tjelmeland, Hallvard, and Grete Brochmann. *Norsk innvandringshistorie I Globaliseringens Tid 1940–2000*. Oslo: Pax Forlag A/S, 2003.

Togeby, Lise. *Fremmedhed og Fremmedhad i Danmark*. Copenhagen: Columbus, 1997.

Udgaard, Nils Morten. *Great Power Politics and Norwegian Foreign Policy*. Oslo: Norwegian University Press, 1973.

United Nations. *Our Common Future*. New York: World Commission on Environment and Development, 1988.

UNU/WIDER. "A Tale of Two Countries: Poverty among Immigrants in Denmark and Sweden since 1984." Discussion Paper No. 2003/36, April 2003, p. 19.

Weber, Steven, ed. *Globalization and the European Political Economy*. New York: Columbia University Press, 2001.

Western Viking. "Bunad Ban Sparks Racism Charges." Vol. 111, no. 40 (November 2000): 7.

Whitehead, Thor. *The Ally Who Came in from the Cold*. Reykjavik: University of Iceland Press, 1998.

Williams, Carol. "Price of Freedom: In Blood." *The Los Angeles Times*, March 7, 2002.

www.britannica.com. "Fridtjof Nansen: Statesman and Humanitarian." Accessed November 29, 2005.

www.nb.no/baser/nansen/english.html. "The Nansen Passport." Accessed November 29, 2005.

www.world-gazetteer.com. "The Population of Scandinavia." Accessed November 29, 2005.

Young, Oran. *Creating Regimes: Arctic Accords and International Governance*. Ithaca, NY: Cornell University Press, 1998.

Index

About the Author

Christine Ingebritsen is associate professor in the Department of Scandinavian Studies, acting dean of Undergraduate Education, and vice provost at the University of Washington in Seattle, Washington. Ingebritsen received her PhD in government from Cornell University and is the author of *The Nordic States and European Unity* (Ithaca, NY: Cornell University Press, 1998 and 2000) and co-editor with Robert Geyer and Jonathan Moses of *Globalization, Europeanization and the End of Scandinavian Social Democracy?* (Basingstoke, UK: Macmillan Press, 2000). She is also co-editor with Sabrina Ramet of *Coming in from the Cold War* (Lanham, MD: Rowman and Littlefield, 2002) and co-editor with Iver Neumann, Sieglinde Gstöhl, and Jessica Beyer of *Small States in International Relations* (Reykjavik and Seattle: University of Iceland and University of Washington Press, 2006).